HAROLD PINTER

The Caretaker

$1.25

With a Commentary and Notes by
PATRICIA HERN

Methuen Student Editions
METHUEN DRAMA

This Methuen Student Edition first published in 1982 by Methuen
London Ltd.
Reprinted 1983
Revised and reprinted 1985, 1987

Reprinted 1988, 1989 by Methuen Drama,
Michelin House, 81 Fulham Road, London SW3 6RB.

The Caretaker first published in 1960 by Methuen & Co.
Revised second edition, 1962.

Printed in Great Britain by
Cox & Wyman Ltd, Reading

ISBN 0 413 49280 X

Contents

Aston (Robert Shaw) and Davies (Donald Pleasence) with Buddha (*above*), and Davies and Mick (Alan Bates) (*below*), both from the 1962 film.

Harold Pinter

1930 10 October. Pinter was born into a Jewish family in
Hackney, an inner suburb in East London. His father was
a tailor, and the family lived in a comfortable terraced
house. Nonetheless, the consciousness of being Jewish and
thus one of a vulnerable group must have been sharpened
by the activities during the 1930s of Oswald Mosley and his
British Union of Fascists.

1939 He was evacuated to Cornwall, returning eventually to
London in 1944, where he attended Hackney Downs
Grammar School, displaying a particular enthusiasm for
English and the theatre.

1948 He gained a grant to attend the Royal Academy of Dramatic
Art, but was unhappy there and left before the end of his
first year.

1948 Pinter was called up for National Service in the Armed
-49 Forces, but, with the fight against Fascism over, he declared
himself a conscientious objector. Two tribunals rejected his
appeal for exemption, but instead of a prison sentence he
escaped with a fine. After taking part in a few radio plays,
he went back to drama school, this time at the Central
School of Speech and Drama.

1951 Pinter was taken on by the actor-manager Anew McMaster
-52 for a Shakespearian tour of Ireland. During this period he
published a number of poems.

1952 Pinter acted in provincial repertory theatre, marrying
-56 actress Vivien Merchant in 1956.

1957 His first play, *The Room,* was produced by Bristol
University Drama Department, then by the Bristol Old Vic
Theatre School whose production brought Pinter to the
attention of a theatre producer, Michael Codron.

1958 Michael Codron bought an option on Pinter's second play,
The Birthday Party. In April, *The Birthday Party* was
performed at the Arts Theatre in Cambridge, toured to
Oxford, Wolverhampton and Brighton, then, in May,
opened at the Lyric Theatre, Hammersmith, in West

London. It closed after only one week, having been savaged by the critics. Only Harold Hobson, drama critic of the Sunday Times, recognised Pinter's quality.

> Mr. Pinter, on the evidence of this work, possesses the most original, disturbing and arresting talent in theatrical London. [. . .] Theatrically speaking *The Birthday Party* is absorbing. It is witty. [. . .] Mr. Pinter has got hold of a primary fact of existence. We live on the verge of disaster.

That winter Pinter wrote another full-length play, *The Hothouse*, but, perhaps discouraged by the initial reception of *The Birthday Party*, he did not submit it for production until 1980.

1959   *The Birthday Party* was performed more successfully by a semi-professional company, the Tavistock Players, at the Tower Theatre in London, and Pinter's radio play, *A Slight Ache,* was broadcast by the BBC.

1960   *The Room and The Dumb Waiter* were produced at the Hampstead Theatre Club, later transferring to the Royal Court Theatre. *A Night Out* was broadcast on radio.

1960   April: *The Caretaker* at the Arts Theatre Club won sufficient critical acclaim to justify its transfer to the Duchess Theatre in the West End, where it ran for a year. *Night School* was televised and another production of *The Birthday Party* opened – this time, in America.

1961   *The Collection* was televised by ATV. *The Caretaker* opened in New York and won good notices.

1962   Pinter wrote the screenplay for Joseph Losey's film of Robin Maugham's novel, *The Servant,* winning the British Screenwriters' Guild Award. *The Caretaker* was filmed.

1963   *The Lover* was televised.

1964   Revival of *The Birthday Party* by the Royal Shakespeare Company at the Aldwych Theatre in June. Directed by Pinter.

1965   Pinter won a British Film Academy Award for his screenplay of Penelope Mortimer's novel, *The Pumpkin Eater. The Homecoming* was presented by the Royal Shakespeare Company at the Aldwych Theatre, London.

1966   The film of Pinter's screenplay, *The Quiller Memorandum,* was directed by Michael Anderson. Pinter was awarded the C.B.E. in the Queen's Birthday Honours List.

1967   *The Basement* was televised by BBC-TV. Pinter wrote the screenplay for Losey's film of *Accident,* a novel by Nicholas Mosley. *The Homecoming* won the Tony Award for the best play on Broadway.

1968   *The Birthday Party* was filmed. Director: William Friedkin.

1969   Pinter completed his adaptation of L.P. Hartley's novel, *The Go-Between,* as a film to be directed by Joseph Losey. Two one-act plays, *Landscape* and *Silence,* were produced by the Royal Shakespeare Company at the Aldwych Theatre. The production on stage of *Landscape* had been delayed because Pinter refused to make the cuts in the text required by the Lord Chamberlain's Office, then still exercising censorship over live theatre. An uncut version of the play, however, had been broadcast on BBC radio in January, 1968.

1971   *Old Times* was presented by the Royal Shakespeare Company at the Aldwych Theatre.

1972   Pinter began work on an adaptation for the screen of Proust's *A la Recherche du Temps Perdu.*

1973   Pinter became an Associate Director at the National Theatre. His short play, *Monologue,* was televised by the BBC.

1975   *No Man's Land* was produced by the National Theatre Company at the Old Vic Theatre, then transferred to the West End, and later was staged in the new National Theatre on London's South Bank.

1978   *Betrayal* opened at the National Theatre.

1980   *The Hothouse,* written in 1958, was directed by Pinter at the Hampstead Theatre, then transferred to the Ambassador's Theatre in the West End. Pinter completed his screenplay of John Fowles' novel, *The French Lieutenant's Woman.* His first marriage ended in divorce; he married Lady Antonia Fraser.

1981   *Family Voices* was broadcast on BBC radio and subsequently staged as a Platform Performance at the National Theatre.

1982   *A Kind of Alaska, Victoria Station* and *Family Voices* staged as a triple-bill entitled *Other Places* at the National Theatre.

1984   *One for the Road* was staged at Lyric Theatre Studio, Hammersmith, directed by Pinter.

1985   *Other Places,* now consisting of *Victoria Station, Family Voices* and *One for the Road,* presented at the Duchess Theatre, London.

Pinter has also directed several of his own plays and plays by other dramatists for the stage and for television, developing a particularly fruitful working relationship with the playwright, Simon Gray.

Plays in order of writing:
*The Room; The Birthday Party; The Dumb Waiter; A Slight Ache;
The Hothouse; A Night Out; The Caretaker; Night School; The
Dwarfs; The Collection; The Lover; Tea Party; The Homecoming;
The Basement; Landscape; Silence; Night; Old Times; Monologue;
No Man's Land; Betrayal; Family Voices; A Kind of Alaska;
Victoria Station, One for the Road.*

Screenplays from other writers' work:
*The Servant; The Pumpkin Eater; The Quiller Memorandum;
Accident; The Go-Between; Langrishe, Go Down; The Last Tycoon;
A la Recherche du Temps Perdu* (not filmed); *The French
Lieutenant's Woman, Turtle Diary.*

Plays directed for the stage:
*The Collection; The Lover; The Dwarfs; The Birthday Party; The
Man in the Glass Booth* by Robert Shaw; *Exiles* by James Joyce;
Butley by Simon Gray; *Next of Kin* by John Hopkins; *Otherwise
Engaged* by Simon Gray; *Blithe Spirit* by Noël Coward; *The
Innocents* by William Archibald; *The Rear Column* by Simon Gray;
Close of Play by Simon Gray; *The Hothouse; Quartermaine's Terms*
by Simon Gray; *Incident at Tulse Hill* by Robert East; *The Trojan
War Will Not Take Place* by Jean Giraudoux; *One for the Road.*

Aston and Davies in a Paris production in 1969 (*Photo: Treatt*)

Plot and structure

'As far as Pinter is concerned, *The Caretaker* is just a play about two brothers and a tramp in a room.' (John Russell Taylor in: *The Playwrights Speak*, p. xiv)

Act One

A man wearing a leather jacket is revealed sitting on a bed in a room which is full of miscellaneous objects: some — like paint buckets and boxes full of nuts and screws, a step-ladder, a blowlamp and some planks of wood — seem to suggest a coherent purpose, but there is also the statue of a Buddha, a shopping trolley, and a number of ornaments piled together on top of a second bed. The man, Mick, sits looking about him, until, at the sound of a door banging and muffled voices, he leaves silently. Aston and Davies come in. Aston's clothes are shabby but neat. Davies's old coat, lack of shirt and general unkemptness proclaim him to be a tramp. He is out of breath and still almost incoherent with outrage at having been set upon in the café where he was working as a cleaner and from which Aston has evidently just rescued him. Aston invites him to stay until he gets himself fixed up elsewhere and they unload the objects from the bed near the window. Aston then offers Davies a small sum of money which the tramp pockets. Davies is in need of a strong pair of shoes to replace his sandals. He is also anxious to recover his bag of belongings left behind at the café. He plans, he says, to journey to Sidcup — an outer suburb to the south east of London, in Kent — once the weather improves. There he hopes to collect papers which he claims will help him prove his official identity and get his life and prospects sorted out. He has, meanwhile, been passing himself off as someone called Jenkins, using a stolen insurance card to support the alias. As Davies takes off his trousers and climbs into bed, he comments unhappily on the bucket hanging above him to catch any water leaking through the roof. Aston sits on his own bed, mending a plug. The light fades.

Next morning Aston is the first to wake. He disturbs Davies who wakes suddenly and with alarm. He vigorously denies Aston's complaint that he has been groaning and talking feverishly in his sleep. He tries to blame the 'Blacks' living next door. Aston prepares to leave, but first gives Davies a doorkey, much to the tramp's surprise. Aston suddenly reminisces about a woman, a stranger he met at a café, who disconcertingly made a pass at him. Davies is anxious about the gas stove near his bed, uncomforted by Aston's assurance that since it is not connected to the gas mains it is perfectly safe. When Aston leaves, Davies tests the key, locks the door, then begins to examine the contents of the room. As he does so, Mick silently enters, pocketing his own key, and takes Davies by surprise, forcing his arm behind his back and pushing him to the floor while Davies struggles and protests. When the tramp is quiet, Mick strips his bed and discovers the trousers. Davies's attempt to rise is blocked by Mick, who then sits in the one chair, surveying the tramp. After a pause, he asks: 'What's the game?'

Act Two

Davies is still on the floor, with Mick seated, watching him. During the following interrogation, Davies tries to bluster but fails to do more than splutter impotently that he is called Jenkins, that he wants his trousers back so that he can set off for Sidcup, and that he is not an intruder but has been invited into the room. Mick alternates between lengthy diatribes, claiming to see likenesses between Davies and his own 'uncle's brother' or another acquaintance, and bursts of quick-fire questioning. He states that the room is his, that it is his bed Davies slept on the previous night and that, indeed, he owns the whole house. He teases Davies who is desperate to reclaim his trousers and thus some shred of dignity. When Aston returns Mick stops baiting Davies, allowing him to grab his trousers and get them on. Aston puts down a bag he has brought in, then begins tinkering with an old toaster. When Davies goes to pick up the bag, claiming it as his, Mick snatches it and begins to goad the old tramp until Aston intervenes. An elaborate game of pig-in-the-middle with the bag follows. Finally Davies secures the bag and retreats to his bed. Mick leaves. In reply to Davies's enquiry, Aston explains that Mick is his brother, that he does in fact own the house and that he himself is supposed to be beginning a scheme of repair and redecoration to the property once he has built himself a shed in the garden to use as a workshop. Davies decides that the disputed bag is not, after all, his. Aston has picked it up somewhere with some clothes in it. He offers Davies

a job as caretaker and cleaner in the house. Davies is wary, nervous
about the kind of caller he might have to deal with, but is
obviously attracted by the suggestion.

A blackout denotes the passage of time, then the lights come up
again very dimly. A key is heard in the lock. Davies enters, barely
perceptible in the gloom. He drops his matches. The sudden
realisation that he is not alone in the room frightens him. He pulls
out a knife defensively, but is terrified by a burst of electrical
noise, the sound of a vacuum cleaner. The sound stops, the light
comes on and Mick is revealed standing on Aston's bed, holding the
plus of the electrolux cleaner. He seems ready to be friendly,
sharing some sandwiches with Davies and confiding his misgivings
about Aston's apparent reluctance to get to work and so make his
way in the world with Mick's help. Mick offers Davies the post as
caretaker, on condition that the tramp can provide acceptable
character references. Davies asserts that he has all the references
necessary — down in Sidcup.

The lights dim; time passes. It is morning. Aston is dressing. He
rouses Davies, reminding him of his intention to go to Sidcup.
Aston is bothered by the noises Davies makes in his sleep. Davies,
however, protests that he cannot sleep because of the cold draught
from the open window near his bed. He shuts the window, despite
Aston's objections. Aston prepares to go out, but mention of a
nearby café leads him to recall times he had spent there in the past,
talking to people about his moments of clear vision — a time
before he was committed, with his mother's complicity, to a
mental institution. His attempt there to avoid electric shock
treatment resulted in permanent damage to his brain and spine,
leaving him slow-thinking, physically clumsy, plagued with head
headaches and shy of human contact. He wants to find the man
responsible for the inhuman treatment, but first he must build his
shed.

Act Three
Two weeks later, Mick and Davies are discovered in the room;
Mick is lying on the floor while Davies sits, apparently at ease, on
the chair, complaining about Aston's behaviour towards him. He
is especially frustrated by Aston's inability or unwillingness to have
what Davies considers a proper conversation. Mick seems more
interested in the possibility of transforming this floor of the house
into a glossy, expensive penthouse apartment, with Davies's help
but apparently no place for the old tramp once the conversion is

complete. He laments Aston's lack of any real interest in such schemes. Davies tries to disclaim any bond with Aston and to ingratiate himself with Mick. He is perturbed by the way he finds Aston smiling at him as he wakes in the mornings. Aston returns, bringing a pair of shoes for Davies, who ungratefully complains that without laces they are no use to him. He grudgingly accepts a pair of brown instead of black laces from Aston, but still finds reasons why he will not be able to set off towards Sidcup the next day.

Night falls. Aston is driven to wake Davies in order to silence his groans. In fury, Davies turns on him, bragging that he and Mick are allies — against Aston if necessary. He threatens Aston with banishment again to a mental hospital and denies that Aston has ever given him any money. Finally he pulls out his knife, nervous that Aston may be provoked to attack him, but Aston merely tells the tramp that it is time he moved on. Relying on his agreement with Mick, Davies defies Aston and even mocks his plans to build a 'stinking shed'. At last Aston is roused to anger and begins to pack Davies's things into his bag. Davies leaves, threatening to summon Mick to deal with Aston.

Next morning Mick and Davies return to an empty room. At first Mick appears sympathetic, but when Davies refers to Aston's time in hospital, he suddenly becomes hostile, accusing Davies of trying to pass himself off as an experienced interior decorator, of being an inveterate liar and no better than an animal. He throws Davies a coin as payment and orders him to leave, then in a burst of anger Mick splinters Aston's statue of Buddha. He is wearied by his responsibilities for the house and decides to leave Aston to do as he wishes with it. Aston returns and Mick leaves without further comment, although the two brothers exchange faint smiles. Aston ignores Davies, beginning to tinker with a plug. Recognising that Mick has rejected him, the tramp tries to salvage his association with Aston. He wheedles, bargains and begs to be allowed to stay. Aston remains unresponsive, finally turning his back on Davies who stands in inarticulate defeat (p. 78):

> DAVIES. . . . Listen . . . if I . . . got down . . . if I was to . . . get my papers . . . would you . . . would you let . . . would you . . . if I got down . . . and got my . . .
>
> *Long silence.*
>
> *Curtain.*

This final image was not Pinter's original idea of the ending:

> 'At the end [. . .] there are two people alone in a room, and one
> of them must go in such a way as to produce a sense of complete
> separation and finality. I thought originally that the play must
> end with the violent death of one at the hands of the other. But
> then I realised, when I got to the point, that the characters as
> they had grown could never act in this way.' (Quoted in John
> Russell Taylor, *Anger and After*, p. 336.)

Davies and Mick in a Tokyo production in 1967.

Commentary

The characters — a question of identity

> The point is, who are you? Not why or how, not even what. I can see what, perhaps, clearly enough. But who are you? [. . .] What you are, or appear to be to me, or appear to be to you, changes so quickly, so horrifyingly, I certainly can't keep up with it and I'm damn sure you can't either.
> (*The Dwarfs*)

The problems of establishing identity, here expressed in Pinter's dramatisation of his novel *The Dwarfs*, are apparent also in *The Caretaker*. The distinction between 'who you are' and 'what you are' is not merely hair-splitting. 'What' can be taken to refer to the confirmable or objective 'fact'; while 'who' can mean the persistent core of the character and what that character may be said to stand for if interpretations are sought. What, for example, is known, or at least apparently true, about Aston, Mick and Davies?

ASTON is in charge of a large house owned by his brother, Mick. Most of the house is unoccupied and all of it is in need of renovation. Aston was once committed to a psychiatric hospital and there given electric shock therapy; now he spends his time collecting miscellaneous objects which appeal to him or which he thinks may prove useful one day. These he stores in his attic bedroom. He plans to build a shed, then, perhaps, redecorate the house.

MICK owns but does not live in this house. He is building up a business which involves ownership of a van.

DAVIES is old. Little is known of his past; that is, little stands independently of his own testimony. When Aston rescues him from a fight at a café, he is out of work and homeless. He has an insurance card in the name of Jenkins but says that it is not his. He has no possessions with him, and his oddly assorted, ill-fitting clothes are evidently other people's cast-offs. He looks like a tramp.

Each of the characters elaborates this outline through his actions, reactions and statements about himself. **Aston** talks of a time, before his shock treatment, when he used to visit a café regularly to talk to people, all older than himself, a time when he worked in a factory and enjoyed communicating with the other workers. 'And these men, they used to listen, whenever I . . . had anything to say. It was all right' (p. 54). But he was troubled by 'kind of hallucinations' or, as he haltingly explains, moments of heightened awareness, visions: 'I used to get the feeling I could see things . . . very clearly . . . everything . . . was so clear . . . everything used . . . everything used to get very quiet . . . everything got very quiet . . . all this . . . quiet . . . and . . . this clear sight . . .' (p. 55). Then, by a process he did not understand, he found himself in a hospital outside London, his attempts to escape blocked, his thoughts investigated, declared somehow unfit, betrayed by his mother, his brain maimed, his senses dulled, his life turned in on itself in retreat from further human contact. His enemies are nameless: 'they' took him to hospital; 'they' asked questions; 'they' came round with the pincers wired into a little machine. 'They' operate within the anonymity of institutions such as the hospital. Aston's struggle to remain intact, himself, seems pathetic yet heroic — the individual against the system. The pathos is heightened by his mother's response to his appeal to her for protection: 'But she signed their form, you see, giving them permission' (p. 56). After so brutal an assault on his identity, on his thoughts and his ability to perceive or respond to the outside world, Aston's continued existence appears only to prolong his suffering. 'The thing is, I should have been dead. I should have died' (p. 57).

In the course of the play he displays gentle kindness and trustfulness, offering Davies shelter, money and a key to the house. He is anxious and distressed by Davies's night-time moaning, and seems to find the old tramp oddly appealing; Davies is disconcerted to wake up in the morning and find Aston standing 'looking at me, smiling!' (p. 63). Finally, when goaded beyond endurance, he reveals a capacity for stolid, sustained anger. His character, on the surface at least, seems unambiguous; there is a consistent connection between the information given about his past and the evidence of his behaviour in the present of the play. He seems to have a future which leads on without violence or absurdity from this observed present: he will continue to inhabit Mick's house and derive hope from his unwavering plans to build a shed.

Mick is the most articulate of the three characters: he uses language as a weapon, both to disarm Davies and to discredit him. Unlike Aston, he offers many shifting perspectives on his past life

and immediate plans. His conversation moves from a quick-fire
questioning of Davies (resembling the interrogation of Stanley by
Goldberg and McCann in *The Birthday Party*) to extended passages
of rhetoric. Compare, for example, the shift from abrupt question
and answer, made disconcerting by the sudden changes of direction
and apparent non sequiturs (pp. 32–3), with the sustained fluency
of his 'No strings attached, open and above board' oration (pp.
35–6). His rhetoric is full of wild juxtapositions (p. 31):

> Had a marvellous stop-watch. Picked it up in Hong Kong. The
> day after they chucked him out of the Salvation Army. Used to
> go in number four for Beckenham Reserves. That was before he
> got his gold medal.

Sometimes the language is full of jargon, the professional phrases
of landlords or estate agents ('I mean it depends whether you
regard this room as furnished or unfurnished' p. 71), of the police
('have you in for trespassing, loitering with intent' p. 36), and
insurance salesmen ('comprehensive indemnity against Riot, Civil
Commotion, Labour Disturbances' p. 36). There are sudden leaps
into the absurd, with half-punning sound-bridges between words:
'loitering with intent' is followed by 'daylight robbery' — the idea
of robbery has a logical connection with the other listed offences,
but 'daylight robbery' suddenly changes the terms of reference
since it is a cliché or idiomatic phrase used to describe any flagrant
and shameless exploitation (not necessarily illegal) of one person
by another. Similarly, he explains that the insurance benefits
offered require a medical certificate to prove that 'you possess the
requisite fitness to carry the can' (p. 36). 'To carry the can' means
to become a scapegoat, to bear the blame for an action for which
one has, probably, only a shared guilt if any at all. The idea of
fitness to carry, say, a heavy weight would be straightforwardly
appropriate within the list; however, the figurative idiom becomes
sinister as well as comic. The appearance of logic gives Mick's set
speeches an air of worldly wisdom and authority, while the sudden
shift into metaphor makes everyday standards of logic or
consistency seem inadequate and absurd. Thus the audience, like
Davies, is left dazzled and disconcerted.

The range of reference, vocabulary and idiom, his knowledge of
London's inner suburbs and bus routes (p. 32), his air of ingenuous
candour ('Uuh . . . listen . . . can I ask your advice? I mean, you're
a man of the world. Can I ask your advice about something?' p.48),
his pretentions to middle-class culture ('You must come up and

have a drink some time. Listen to some Tchaikovsky' p. 64) and
to the trappings of bourgeois affluence, expressed in the language
of advertising copy (p. 60), together with his abrupt crudities ('you
stink from arse-hole to breakfast time' p. 74) all combine to give an
impression of mercurial elusiveness to Mick. He seems to assume
subtly different identities with shifting references which undermine
any attempt to define *who* he is. He has a strange trick of echoing
words spoken by the others earlier when he was not present; for
instance, in Act One Davies talks furiously of the man who tried
to attack him – he is speaking to Aston: 'The filthy skate, an old
man like me, I've had dinner with the best' (p. 9). In Act Two
Mick hurls the same insult at Davies: 'You're an old skate. You
don't belong in a nice place like this' (p. 35). When Aston and
Davies are alone, Aston offers the old man the job of caretaker in
the house (p. 42):

ASTON. You could be . . . caretaker here, if you liked.
DAVIES. What?
ASTON. You could . . . look after the place, if you liked . . .
you know, the stairs and the landing, the front steps, keep an
eye on it.

In the next encounter between Mick and Davies, Mick makes the
same suggestion (p. 50):

MICK. How would you like to stay on here, as caretaker?
DAVIES. What?
MICK. I'll be quite open with you. I could rely on a man like
you around the place, keeping an eye on things.

Yet Mick, like Aston, can be taken on a naturalistic level: he
belongs to a tradition of sharp London lads on the make, from
under-privileged or working-class backgrounds, who acquire
material possessions and social mobility through their native wit
and their ability to recognise and to play the rules of the system,
picking up their jargon, their attitudes and their affectations from
radio, television, the popular press and the middle-class professions
whose world impinges on theirs – the Law, the police, property
investments, insurance (p. 74):

I got plenty of other interests. I've got my own business to
build up, haven't I? I got to think about expanding . . . in all
directions. I don't stand still. I'm moving about, all the time.

In an interview given in 1966 and published in the *Paris Review* in 1967, Pinter described one of the starting points for the character of **Davies**:

> I met a few, quite a few tramps — you know, just in the normal course of events — and I think there was one particular one [. . .] I didn't know him very well; he did most of the talking when I saw him. I bumped into him a few times, and about a year or so afterwards he sparked this thing off.

This is to say, on this occasion, as with *The Room* and *The Birthday Party*, Pinter began with the character, from an encounter with the real, physical world, *not* with a commitment to an idea or a philosophy. He made this point also in an interview given to the *New Yorker*, 25 February 1967:

> I regard myself as an old-fashioned writer. I like to create character and follow a situation to its end.

Davies's predicament in the play is bound up with the question of identity posed at the beginning of this section: 'The point is, who are you?' Answers commonly begin with references to an individual's place within recognisable social groups or categories — as father of a family, or the product of parents from a particular race, district and social class, shaped by a particular education system (probably also related to his social class), trained for a particular career or profession, perhaps brought up within one of the mainstream religions, given the official tag of a National Insurance number, a birth certificate and, finally, a death certificate. A name and a set of facts. In his poem 'The Unknown Citizen' W.H. Auden demonstrated through an ironic epitaph dedicated to Mr. Average, a twentieth-century Everyman, that such data provide only a superficial, even misleading account of a man's identity and worth, but statistics and social groupings can at least require general recognition of a style of life, a function within the group, a verifiable sequence of events. If none, or few, of these points of reference exist clearly, how then does an individual define himself?

Davies has scraps of memory and an array of responses from which to patch together a picture of himself. He needs to assemble that image himself since he has no-one who is close enough to do it for him. He feels alone and vulnerable, so must defend his own space and feel the fight justified by his own worth. He claims to have had 'dinner with the best', whoever they might be (p. 9). He prides himself on his personal cleanliness ('I might have been on the road a few years but you can take it from me I'm clean. I keep myself up' p. 9). He recalls the time when his youth and vigour ensured that 'they didn't take any liberties' with him (p. 9). He was 'brought up with the right ideas' (p. 10) and knows he has rights, even if he cannot define them clearly. He has papers, he says, to prove who he is, with plenty of references to establish his good character (p. 51), a 'capable sort of man' (p. 50), who has had 'plenty of offers' (p. 50) and has, perhaps, been in the services ('Overseas . . . like . . . serving . . . I was' p. 50). His language here is ambiguous. One 'serves' in the Armed Forces, certainly, but one also 'serves' a prison sentence. Mick's suggestion that Davies's serving was 'in the colonies' calls to mind Britain's former habit of transporting convicted criminals to penal settlements in her colonies, to Botany Bay in Australia, for instance.

Davies's reminiscences cohere to form a credible character: he talks of his travels from Luton (a town some 30 miles north of London) to the northern and western suburbs of the capital, such as Watford, Hendon, Wembley, Shepherd's Bush; he mentions a variety of temporary jobs, all commonly open to casual and unskilled labour like Davies ('cleaning the floor, clearing up the tables, doing a bit of washing-up' p. 9). His prejudices quite reasonably can be seen to grow out of his insecurity about his social status; he feels the need to assert his superiority over those aliens and immigrants who he feels usurp his rights and invade his territory (p. 8):

> All them Blacks had it, Blacks, Greeks, Poles, the lot of them, that's what, doing me out of a seat, treating me like dirt.

He is aggressively insistent about his sense of what is 'proper' (p. 10):

> Look here, I said, I'm an old man, I said, where I was brought up we had some idea how to talk to old people with the proper respect, we was brought up with the right ideas. [. . .] I might have been on the road but nobody's got more rights than I have.

As a tramp, Davies exists on the fringes of society, parasitically: he depends upon the machinery and the benefits of a welfare state and organised charities while evading the shared responsibilities or obligations to society which such benefits imply. Up until this century he would have been described under the terms of the

English Poor Law as 'one of the undeserving poor', thought of as shiftless idlers who were to be discouraged from resting upon the charity of others by being treated with hostility and harshness when they looked for food, clothing or shelter. It can be an emotive issue in literature when the writer's commitment to one or other side is strongly presented. In novels, for instance, such as *Oliver Twist* and *Hard Times*, the Victorian novelist, Charles Dickens, showed organised welfare — whether by local government or so-called philanthropic societies — as grudging, inadequate and inhumane, an affront to the right of every man, no matter how poor or pathetic, to his dignity, his self-respect and his pursuit of happiness.

Davies is personally unappealing: his blustering arrogance, his intolerance, his selfishness, his ingratitude and his treachery make it easy to feel indignation at his exploitation and abuse of others. It is, arguably, *his* fault that he is alone, penniless, homeless and afraid; society is not to blame. The play shows him reacting to the offer of shelter and an occupation with increasing gracelessness, culminating in his violent abuse of Aston during which he pulls out a knife (pp. 66—8). Should one feel sympathy for this character who can so viciously turn against his benefactor, using as a weapon his knowledge of Aston's deepest horror and fears? Balanced against this is Davies's own terror, his sense of existing hand to mouth in an antagonistic world where all is suspect, calculated either to discount or to destroy him. He feels perpetually like an animal at bay, menaced by 'Poles, Greeks, Blacks, the lot of them' (p. 8), by an aggressive Scotsman (p. 10), a slatternly wife (p. 9), by uncharitable monks (pp. 14—5), by the machinery of government (p. 20), by 'any Harry' who might be on the doorstep (pp. 43—4), by Mick's games of menace (p. 34 and p. 45), even by Aston's secret smiling (p. 63). Yet the idea of being like an animal, in any way, undermines his precarious sense of his own human dignity. 'Treating me like a bloody animal!' (p. 67); 'Meal? I said, what do you think I am, a dog? Nothing better than a dog. What do you think I am, a wild animal?' (p. 15).

At the beginning of Act Two, Mick jabs at the tramp's uncertainties: 'What's your name?' (p. 30). 'You a foreigner?' 'Born and bred in the British Isles?' 'What did they teach you?' (p. 33). When Davies stumblingly offers answers, Mick rejects them and passes judgement on who and what Davies is: 'I'm afraid you're a born fibber' (p. 34). 'You're an old robber, there's no getting away from it. You're an old skate. You don't belong in a nice place like this. You're an old barbarian' (p. 35). Having teased, tempted and observed Davies, Mick maintains that experience has tested and confirmed this description of who the man is, a wholesale denial of the claims Davies has made for himself (pp. 73—4).

> MICK. What a strange man you are. Aren't you? You're really strange. Ever since you came into this house there's been nothing but trouble. Honest. I can take nothing you say at face value. Every word you speak is open to any number of different interpretations. Most of what you say is lies. You're violent, you're erratic, you're just completely unpredictable. You're nothing else but a wild animal, when you come down to it. You're a barbarian.

The fact that Davies is vague about his own origins (p.25) and evasive when directly questioned about his past (p. 50) does not undermine the credibility or validity of the character. It is arguably more 'realistic' than the more conventional or traditional approach which allows characters to speak with authority and clarity about who they are and where they come from, even why they are behaving as they are. In an address to students at Bristol in 1962 (reprinted as the introduction to *Pinter Plays: One*), Pinter defended his own approach to characterisation:

> The desire for verification is understandable, but cannot always be satisfied. There are no hard distinctions between what is real and what is unreal, nor between what is true and what is false. [. . .] A character on the stage who can present no convincing argument or information as to his past experiences, his present behaviour or his aspirations, nor give a comprehensive analysis of his motives, is as legitimate and as worthy of attention as one who, alarmingly, can do all these things.

Quite apart from a character's wish to conceal his past or his personal identity from others on the grounds that an open confession might incriminate him, there is the difficulty of being sure that what one remembers at any one moment is the truth, the whole truth and nothing but the truth. Davies is, however, aware of the need for some evidently reliable endorsement of those rights which he so vehemently asserts. In an age of bureaucracy, official recognition and guarantees are necessary, even if, to a man of the tramp's limited education and narrow understanding, the precise form this should take is uncertain (p. 20):

> You see? They prove who I am! I can't move without them
> papers. They tell you who I am. You see! I'm stuck without
> them.

He fears discovery and punishment for trying to cheat the system
(p. 20):

> That's not my real name, they'd find out, they'd have me in the
> nick.

He is afraid of being destitute, isolated, adrift, so struggles to
establish his place in Mick's house, trying to play one brother off
against the other. When Mick passionately exclaims that he has no
further interest in the house so will leave Aston to do what he likes
with it, Davies asks anxiously: 'What about me?' (p. 61). As Aston
stands silently excluding him at the end of the play, he protests
(p. 77):

> 'What am I going to do?
>
> *Pause.*
>
> What shall I do?
>
> *Pause.*
>
> Where am I going to go?'

Slice of Life? Poetic reality? Theatre of the Absurd?

In the late 1950s plays set in Home Counties drawing-rooms or
famous historical periods were being pushed off the London stage
by a new fashion for what became known as 'kitchen sink' drama
— described disparagingly by the polished playwright Noël Coward
as the 'scratch and mumble school'. The reaction against comedies
of upper-middle-class manners (plays, for example, by Rattigan or
Coward, or dramatised from Agatha Christie), against revivals of
the classics and elegant excursions into verse drama by dramatists
such as T.S. Eliot or Christopher Fry, and against sentimental
musicals (like *The Boyfriend* by Sandy Wilson and *Salad Days* by
Julian Slade) was given vivid and successful expression in John
Osborne's play, *Look Back in Anger*, which was produced at the
Royal Court Theatre, London, in 1956. The opening stage
direction reads:

> The scene is a fairly large attic room, at the top of a large Victorian house.

The play provoked extreme reactions but, significantly, men of influence and authority in 1956, such as the American dramatist Arthur Miller and young directors like Tony Richardson and Lindsay Anderson, hailed it as:

> Modern in the sense that the basic attention in the play was found in the passionate idea of the man involved and of the playwright involved, and not toward the surface glitter and amusement that the situation might throw off.
> (Arthur Miller, *Encore*, November 1956)

The movement was extended through the work of writers such as Arnold Wesker, Bernard Kops, Shelagh Delaney and Ann Jellicoe, and became known as 'The New Wave'. It was particularly associated with the Royal Court Theatre in London. In September, 1959, another young dramatist, John Whiting, described the aims and idiom of this movement.

> It may be said that the theatre is compelled to present its conclusions more in terms of feeling than of reason. [. . .] In the matter of style, the movement is largely committed to realism. Reality, I suppose, may be defined as applying to any one person all that comes within that person's experience.
> (*Encore*, September 1959)

Thus, by 1960 audiences were unlikely to be startled or offended by the opening images of *The Caretaker* — a cluttered, cheerless room at the top of a large Victorian or Edwardian house. The window lets in draughts, the roof leaks, the air is cold. The neighbouring houses contain immigrant families. It is an area of large houses, either split up into flatlets and bed-sitters or decaying gloomily — characteristic of many of London's once affluent Victorian and Edwardian suburbs.

It is, however, important to remember that also in the late fifties and sixties other forms of drama moved into the London theatre. In 1956 the Berliner Ensemble visited London for the first time with plays by Bertolt Brecht, introducing a new style of performance and an abrasive, explicit social or political message. George Devine, first artistic director of the English Stage Company at the Royal Court Theatre, wrote enthusiastically:

> A form of poetic reality is presented to them [the audience] for

their consideration. [. . .] You are not told that this is life, that this is really happening. Rather, these are actors presenting a tale for you to witness, for you to form your own conclusions about.
(*Encore*, April 1956)

In 1955 the Arts Theatre Club in London presented *The Lesson* by the Rumanian-born playwright, Ionesco, and *Waiting for Godot* by the Anglo-Irish novelist, poet and dramatist, Samuel Beckett. Richard Roud, a theatre critic writing in *Encore* in 1958, saw these plays as part of the avant-garde movement blossoming then in France (both Ionesco and Beckett lived in Paris) which was 'characterised by its attempts to express metaphysical ideas in concrete theatrical terms'. That is to say, they dealt with abstract concepts rather than being occupied by the visible and familiar processes of day-to-day living.

> Exactly when did the gods retire from the world, exactly when did the images lose their colour? Exactly when was the world emptied of substance, exactly when were the signs no longer signs, exactly when did the gods no longer want to stage a spectacle, exactly when did they no longer want us as spectators, as participants? We were abandoned to ourselves, to our solitude, to our fear, and the problem was born. What is this world? Who are we?
> (*Present Past Past Present: thoughts and memoirs of Eugene Ionesco*, Calder and Boyars, 1973, p. 116)

This drama aspires to universality, yet uses actors, gestures and props which are necessarily *not* abstractions but specific and individualised, and which can engage the spectators' feelings as well as challenge their philosophies. The longing for answers and the final 'I don't know' were given a dramatic life in Ionesco's play, *The Chairs* (1952), in which an old couple — caretakers, perhaps — set out chairs for those who will come (but remain unseen) to hear an orator deliver the old man's message 'for all men, for all mankind'. The orator arrives but is unable to speak. In *The New Tenant*, 1957, Ionesco shows a man taking possession of an empty room, then deliberately allowing himself to be buried beneath a mountain of furniture brought in by removal men. The spectacle is both absurd and disturbing. Ionesco, again (p. 81):

> The most absurd thing is to be conscious of the fact that human existence is unbearable, that the human condition is unbearable,

intolerable, and nonetheless cling desperately to it, knowing and complaining that one is going to lose what is unbearable.

This absurdity suffuses Beckett's play, *Waiting for Godot*. Two tramps, Vladimir and Estragon, try to while away the hours they must spend waiting for the mysterious Godot to come and give their lives meaning or purpose. They try to remember the past, they tell jokes, they argue, occasionally they are silent. Underlying their words is always an undercurrent of panic, of growing frustration, of near despair. Godot does not come. They are stranded in a stark, unspecific landscape — but there is a road and a tree, recognisable features — in an unspecified year, but time does pass, night falls, day dawns, the tree breaks into leaf.

Pinter's play, *The Caretaker*, coming in 1960, straddles these dramatic genres: on the one hand, a theatre of feeling committed to realism; on the other form of poetic reality, absurd yet mordant. Pinter himself has always resisted any attempt to place him wholly within one particular movement or to attach a definitive label to his work.

> Sometimes I feel absurd and sometimes I don't. But I know that life isn't, and my plays are not either. I'm trying to get to this fairly recognisable reality of the absurdity of what we do and how we behave and how we speak.
> (Interview in the *Paris Review*, 1967)

Unlike Beckett's clown-tramps in *Waiting for Godot*, Pinter's characters inhabit a deliberately specific place and period; they appear first as 'people, who come into a particular situation' (Introduction to *Pinter Plays: Two*), a situation which the audience is invited to share through sympathetically witnessing the play's performance. *Later* they may be seen as demonstrating the playwright's view of Man and Life. In a 1960 interview with Kenneth Tynan, Pinter said:

> I mean, there comes a point, surely, where this living in *the* world must be tied up with living in *your own* world, where you are — in your room. [. . .] Before you manage to adjust yourself to living alone in your room [. . .] you are not terribly fit and equipped to go out and fight the battles [. . .] which are fought mostly in abstractions in the outside world.
> (Quoted in Esslin, *Pinter: A Study of his Plays*, p. 34)

Some critics in 1960 saw only what was familiar in *The Caretaker*

and not what was original. Patrick Gibbs, for example, wrote in
The Daily Telegraph:

> . . . had *Waiting for Godot* never been written this piece would
> be judged masterly. As it is it appeared to be excessively
> derivative, almost to the point of parody.

Parody? This implies that *The Caretaker* is a burlesque imitation of
Beckett's play. Certainly there are echoes, both in the patterns of
language and in some of the characters' problems. For example,
Beckett's tramp, Estragon, has difficulties with his boots: they
don't fit properly; they lack suitable laces (*Waiting for Godot*,
Faber, p. 69). Davies, too, is troubled by shoes that are too tight
and have no acceptable laces (p. 64). In *Waiting for Godot*
Estragon and Vladimir perform a comic routine involving the
passing backwards and forwards of three hats (pp. 71–2). In *The
Caretaker* Aston, Mick and Davies pass a bag backwards and
forwards in a similarly complicated, and possibly comic, routine
(p. 39). Estragon and Vladimir develop a refrain which becomes
more poignant with each repetition, conveying their need to act
yet their inability to take the first decisive step themselves (p. 48):

> ESTRAGON. Let's go.
> VLADIMIR. We can't.
> ESTRAGON. Why not?
> VLADIMIR. We're waiting for Godot.

Davies also talks of 'going' yet fails to make his way (p. 16):

> DAVIES. And I'll have to be moving about, you see, try to get
>   fixed up.
> ASTON. Where you going to go?
> DAVIES. Oh, I got one or two things in mind. I'm waiting for
>   the weather to break.

Then, later (p. 63):

> DAVIES. I got business to see to. I got to move myself, I got to
>   sort myself out, I got to get fixed up. But when I wake up in
>   the morning, I ain't got no energy in me. And on top of that
>   I ain't got no clock.

Both acts of *Waiting for Godot* end with the tramps agreeing to
leave, but remaining still (p. 94):

> VLADIMIR. Well? Shall we go?

ESTRAGON. Yes, let's go.

They do not move.

Similarly, the final image of *The Caretaker* is Aston standing impassively, with Davies paralysed by fear and hope (p. 78):

DAVIES. If you want me to go . . . I'll go. You just say the word.

Pause.

We do not see him leave.

Pinter has also spoken of the effect Beckett's novels had on him as a young man. *Murphy*, for example, deals with a highly articulate, eccentric Irishman living on the fringes of London society with an increasing lack of involvement in that materialistic, busy world until he retreats into a 'genuine garret' in a mental hospital. This novel was first published in Britain in 1938. The way in which Beckett shows the distinction between the mad and the supposedly sane as seemingly arbitrary and the petty routines or preoccupations of conventional living as absurd, the flights of rhetoric punctuated by sudden banality, and the precise placing of people and events in recognisable settings where the attention to detail is so meticulous as to be disturbing — all this finds echoes in Pinter's work. *Malone Dies* (published in translation from the French in 1958), traces the dying thoughts of an old man, alone in a room. Malone's sense of his individuality is as insistent and fragmented as Davies's, projected in part through mournful stories about a tramp called Macmann who might represent Malone when younger.

He will therefore rise, whether he likes it or not, and proceed by other places to another place, and then by others still to yet another, unless he comes back here where he seems to be snug enough, but one never knows, does one? And so on, on, for long years.

To accept that *The Caretaker* has points of contact with *Waiting for Godot* and Beckett's novels is to place Pinter within a European tradition leading back at least to the Czech writer Franz Kafka (1883–1924), an influence acknowledged by Pinter. K, the central character of Kafka's novel, *The Trial*, has a kinship with Stanley in Pinter's first full-length play, *The Birthday Party*; they are both the victims of two menacing strangers who invade their private world with accusations of unspecified crimes against humanity, society and, possibly, the state. Kafka's diaries show an anxiety about problems of definition, the tendency of words to take on a life and significance independent of the writer's intentions, and about the spurious authority granted to author's comments on their own works — all anxieties expressed by Pinter in essays and interviews.

'What meaning have yesterday's conclusions today?' writes Kafka (*Diaries*, Peregrine Books, 1964, p. 400). In *The Trial* and *The Castle* Kafka's characters try to grapple with an elusive but implacable machinery of government or bureaucracy which confuses, frustrates and undoes them. Aston and Davies also live in the shadow of the anonymous but powerful 'they' who could have Davies 'in the nick' for carrying false papers and who were responsible for Aston's sufferings in a mental institution.

Pinteresque

In *Brief Chronicles*, Martin Esslin explained his view of Pinter's relationship to Kafka and Beckett: 'Realism and the absurd are fused in a different way', both in the language and the plots, 'where the strictest application of realism produces a feeling of the fantastic and the absurd' (p. 231). Peter Hall, who has directed a number of Pinter's plays to considerable critical acclaim, talked to Irving Wardle, drama critic of *The Times*, about the challenge provided by the ambiguities and the unexpected in Pinter's plays:

> The only kind of theatre that's really interesting is something which is, in the proper sense of the term, poetic.
> (Casebook on *The Homecoming*, John and Anthea Lahr, Davis-Poynter, 1974, p. 19)

To argue that a play is 'poetic' is to draw attention to its high degree of organisation along lines other than narrative, to suggest that the language is likely to be full of imagery, perhaps woven into the character-play and more conventionally functional dialogue, and that the words and gestures may be charged with heightened emotion or thematic significance which transcends the specific situations of the plot. It is to invite interpretations and the search for symbols. Pinter has also, however, been placed within the tradition of English high comedy, that is, comedy which depends upon verbal wit and the precise mockery of society's manners and affectations rather than upon slapstick clowning and ludicrously exaggerated escapades.

The fact that he can quite legitimately be related to Kafka and Beckett on the one hand, and to Oscar Wilde and Nöel Coward on the other, is highly characteristic of Pinter's originality, his ability to work on a multiplicity of different levels.
(Esslin, p. 49).

So what does the term 'Pinteresque' mean? It describes a style of play-writing where the dialogue appears to use the clichés and patterns of everyday conversation to express a darker sense of man's insecurity, aggressiveness or hypocrisy. Perfectly ordinary place-names become absurd when Pinter presents them in an incongruous or unexpected context. Sidcup, for example, is not in itself any more absurd than any other middle-sized town within commuting distance of London; it might even be said to epitomise middle class orthodoxy. Yet it becomes absurd as the apparently unattainable goal towards which Davies claims to be striving in his quest for security and peace of mind. The unexpectedness of Sidcup as Davies's Shining City is emphasised by Aston's response (p. 19). The sound of a commonplace domestic gadget, a vacuum cleaner, becomes terrifying because it erupts into the darkness which is already charged with menace (p. 45). Taking away a man's trousers to leave him without dignity is a stock device in farce; when Mick takes possession of the tramp's trousers, however, it becomes an act of aggressive domination, a ritual of humiliation which makes the slapstick clowning fraught with tension.

There is the repetition of phrases, at first perhaps trite, but becoming more telling with each utterance — sometimes revealing a character's private nightmare or ambition, sometimes using the inconsequential nature of the phrase itself as a reflection of the emotional or intellectual poverty of the speaker. Conversations occur where characters use stock phrases to escape the need to take real account of each other's demands, to ward off questions. This can be seen in the encounter between Davies and Mick at the beginning of Act Two. Yet Pinter denied that his plays were about failure of communication.

I believe the contrary. I think that we communicate only too well, in our silence, in what is unsaid, and that what takes place is a continual evasion, desperate rearguard attempts to keep ourselves to ourselves.
(Introduction to *Pinter Plays: One*).

This pressure to retreat from telling the whole truth, or from hearing the whole truth, makes sudden bursts of honesty, betrayal or accusation, all the more startling. The pauses which Pinter deliberately calls for should never be seen merely as stopping places, empty spaces, but eloquent, revealing more about a character's anxieties or needs than words are allowed to.

Eloquent pauses, self-betrayal through unfinished phrases, and the shock of sudden, extended utterance are all important features of *The Caretaker*. In the final exchange between Davies and Aston, the pauses are resonant with the tramp's urgent need to re-establish himself and Aston's refusal to allow him a foothold (p. 75). Davies insinuates, then is driven to beg, his growing terror communicated through the breakdown of his language: 'But . . . but . . . look . . . listen . . listen here . . . I mean . . .' (p. 77). In contrast to this is Aston's unexpected outpouring of remembered betrayal and suffering at the end of Act Two (pp. 54–7). The passage is startling partly because so sustained, but nonetheless appears painfully authentic as Aston searches for words to match his memories, tentatively. Pinter's organisation of the language — pauses, repetitions, hesitations, spasms of coherent certainty — makes the speech an effectively dramatic climax to the act, even though there is little physical movement called for, and the room grows steadily darker, focusing the audience's attention on the pattern of words and giving Aston's final statement great force (p. 57):

> I don't talk to anyone . . . like that. I've often thought of going back and trying to find the man who did that to me. But I want to do something first. I want to build that shed out in the garden.

Structure

Like Pinter's first full-length play, *The Birthday Party*, *The Caretaker* is organised into three acts. However, there are significant differences. *The Birthday Party* deals with one point of crisis, with the action concentrated within a twenty-four hour span: Act One contains the exposition, introducing the characters, demonstrating their relationship to each other, and announcing the key event, the party itself, which will move the plot towards its central crisis; Act Two builds quickly to the dramatic climax, the amount of explicit conflict after which nothing will ever be quite the same; Act Three shows the repercussions of that event — the characters have all been changed by the experience. *The Caretaker*, on the other hand, shows a process of gradually increasing tension and shifting alliances, extended over a period of more than two weeks. Each act contains a series of episodes, some defined by the falling of darkness, others by the entry or departure of one of the characters.

The play's opening — Mick's silent presence and quick exit from the attic room — acts as a kind of prologue, planting the suggestion of future conflict or menace, or possibly merely complication, in the mind of the audience, which then casts shadows over the next episode, the introductions and explanations between Aston and Davies. Certainly Act One fulfils the functions of a conventional exposition: the three characters are presented, a relationship between them explained, the basis of the action defined — the tramp's entry into the brothers' territory. Act One also demonstrates the range of mood and style to be developed through the play, and contains many of the recurrent concerns — identity, status, invasion and defence of territory, trust and betrayal.

Act Two begins — as does Act Two of *The Birthday Party* — with an interrogation full of menace, and at the same time comic, punctuated by displays of physical aggression that do not in fact result in injury. The end of the episode is marked by the change of rhythm and the lowering of the dramatic intensity with Aston's return, leading to a further set of explanations which in part answer questions posed by Mick's intervention in the action. The nature of Davies's relationship to the others is altered by Aston's suggestion that he become caretaker of the property; this is a significant plot development although not itself obviously a dramatic high point. This episode ends as the light fades. The next is a second encounter between Mick and Davies; like the first, it begins challengingly, the possibility of danger strongly felt. By the end of the episode, Mick has complicated the picture of his motivations and mood while apparently confirming the tramp's transition from the role of outsider to one of the household. The lights dim again and attention then shifts to Aston, bringing him into sharper focus by revealing a crucial aspect of his past experience.

In Act Three the balanced pattern of exchanges between each of the brothers and the tramp continues, working rather like a series of arias, duets and trios in an opera where themes are stated and developed, the key changed, and variations introduced within a clearly defined formal structure. The quality of the relationships changes — exploration and testing of the boundaries develop into more overt competition for space and status as Davies tries to conspire with one brother against the other, then to reverse alliances, as he struggles to possess and hold a position within the house. Just as there is no one, indisputable crisis point or pivot for the action in *The Caretaker* — unlike *The Birthday Party* — so too the ending is less clear-cut. *The Birthday Party* ends when the intruders, Goldberg and McCann, leave Meg's boarding house, taking their victim with them. At the end of *The Caretaker*, Davies hovers on the brink of expulsion; Aston remains unyielding — the resolution of this situation is not shown.

Themes and interpretations

Looking beyond *The Caretaker* simply as a social document, more allegorical or symbolic elements have been discerned in the play. The urge to interpret and explain, to delve below the surface of the action to discover signs and symbols, flies in the face of Pinter's assertion in a 1961 interview reprinted as the Introduction to *Pinter Plays: Two* that:

> I certainly don't write from any kind of abstract idea. And I wouldn't know a symbol if I saw one. I don't see that there's anything very strange about *The Caretaker*, for instance, and I can't quite understand why so many people regard it in the way they do. It seems to me a very straightforward and simple play.

In his 1962 lecture to students at Bristol, Pinter represented the desire to discuss character and dramatic action in abstract terms as a retreat from direct, personal involvement: a neatly structured concept or modernised myth is less challenging and disturbing than a character or an event which might be drawn from or presently intrude upon the audience's 'real life' experiences. In a review of *The Caretaker* at the National Theatre in 1980, Benedict Nightingale briskly catalogued a few of the more popular views of the play, before describing his own response:

> *The Caretaker* has long proved a provocation to academic critics, who have found it hard to explain why so seemingly simple a piece should be so potent in both study and theatre, and have therefore sought solace in one far-fetched interpretation after another. The tramp Davies is Dionysus, or the Wandering Jew, or maybe the tempter in a modern *Everyman* play, or conceivably Everyman himself, beset by a dark angel and a bright angel, namely the brothers Mick and Aston. Or perhaps Aston is the carpenter Christ, building his Church in the form of the garden shed that so obsesses him. Or perhaps, at some

profounder level, the play involves the Old Testament God, the New Testament God and suffering humanity, though which character is supposed to represent which I have thankfully forgotten. Pinter's own comments on it have all been characteristically unpretentious, and I, for one, don't think him disingenuous. If *The Caretaker* is 'about' anything (and only our modern mania for abstraction obliges it to be) it might almost be about methods of eviction.
(*New Statesman*, 21.11.1980)

The suggestion that the play has mythic qualities implies that it is a story which gives expression to — rather than explains — widely shared human experiences, fears and aspirations which cannot adequately be presented through philosophical debate or ethical analysis. It is, perhaps, an enactment of the Freudian compulsion in a son to displace his father, as Martin Esslin suggests: '*The Caretaker* works most forcefully as a dream, a myth of the explusion of the Father by the Sons' (*Brief Chronicles* p. 224). Aston can be seen to feel a filial responsibility for Davies: he collects the old man's bag from the café, he provides shoes for him, he brings him into his home, but finally decides that he must reject Davies in order to complete his own growth (p. 77). Mick claims to see familiar features in Davies: 'You remind me of my uncle's brother' (p. 31). His father, then? He asks the old man for advice as 'a man of the world', then claims to feel betrayed by 'the only man I've told about my dreams, about my deepest wishes' (p. 72) and finally turns him out, offering him a token payment for caretaking.

Davies himself has been seen as a personification of human weakness: he is full of pride, greed, selfish cruelty, treachery and terror. Because of his frailties and follies he forfeits his place in the haven of the house; he is driven from Eden like the Old Testament Adam, to face pain, sickness, death. He acts out the fable of the Camel's Nose — the animal who bargains his way out of a sandstorm into the nomad's tent until finally he displaces his benefactor. Davies, however, miscalculates and by pushing in too far loses his initial advantage, arguably a comment on the twentieth century Human Condition as Man colonises and abuses his environment until it becomes unable to support him longer.

Aston's persecution at the hands of society because of his 'kind of hallucinations', his moments of clear sight, places him in the line of seers, artists and dreamers maimed or martyred for their visions, both in history and in fiction. He perhaps represents the extension of an idea discernible in *The Birthday Party*; there Stanley, a musician, is forced by two sinister intruders to conform to the materialistic society which he has tried to reject — or rather, that is a possible interpretation of the events of the play. In *The Caretaker*, on the other hand, it is ordinary people in café and factory who are Aston's 'persecutors'. They feel compelled to silence him, to 'do something' to his brain, using the machinery and expertise of socially approved institutions. Responsibility for Aston's suffering is therefore shared by anyone living without protest in a society that makes such things possible, who accepts that it is in everyone's best interests that he should 'live like the others'. When he struggles to remain intact, they dislocate his perception of the world and effectively take away his voice. This is, then, a play concerned with communal guilt arising from violence, violence as defined by the French poet, actor and director, Antonin Artaud (1866—1948) in the manifesto for his Theatre of Cruelty: 'Violence consists in depriving a person of his autonomy and of his freedom of choice'.

Professor Konrad Lorenz in his book *On Aggression* (London, Methuen, 1966) progressed from a study of aggression and appeasement patterns in animals, linked to the demands of territorial possession and self-preservation, to a view of human behaviour as displaying essentially the same patterns, although sometimes in a more oblique or sophisticated form. The importance of territory and the manner of a man's response to intrusion from outside have been commented on in a number of Pinter's plays, for example, *The Basement* and *The Homecoming*. The rituals of threat, appeasement, retreat, defence, and the shifting strategy of confrontation have the power to involve an audience because they appeal to deeply rooted responses which are universal and have little to do with education or an enthusiasm for dramatic theory and philosophical debate. Aston brings Davies into his space. At first Davies is visibly uneasy, watchful, defensive, conscious of being within the boundaries of another man and uncertain, therefore, as to his safety and how to signal correctly that he is not an enemy but a potential ally. When yet another contender for this space ritualistically threatens Davies, the tramp is helpless because not on his own ground, not defending his own territory. He does not become effectively hostile himself until he feels cornered and begins to fight for survival. Like an animal, also, he marks out his new — or hoped for — territory by rearranging elements within it, moving objects, imprinting it with his smell.

This is not to say, however, that Pinter deliberately set out to dramatise Darwin or Lorenz or Freud. In his speech to the students at Bristol in 1962, he emphasised that he began his plays in what he called 'quite a simple manner'. He had usually 'found a couple of characters in a particular context, thrown them together and listened to what they said'. *The Caretaker* is evidently susceptible to religious, symbolic, metaphysical or biological interpretations, but it can also be seen as the dramatic presentation of a number of concerns and anxieties endured by twentieth-century urban man. There is, for example, the strain and difficulties of coping with a handicapped member of the family: Mick's energies are divided between trying to build up his own business and worrying about how to provide security and a way of life for Aston since Aston cannot cope with the outside world. Davies has no home, no family, no steady employment; somehow he has slipped through the mesh of the welfare state. He is also haunted by anxiety about time (p. 62):

DAVIES: I mean, if you can't tell what time you're at you
     don't know where you are, you understand my meaning?
     [...] No, what I need is a clock in here, in this room, and
     then I stand a bit of a chance.

What might at first seem just another example of the tramp's confused, laughable superstitions, becomes less absurd in the context of a society conditioned by the demands of time-keeping — clocking in and out of work, adapting to the routines of railway timetables and professional appointments, separating free time from working hours. The English language is heavy with time references: 'All in good time.' 'A stitch in time saves nine.' 'Time and tide wait for no man.' 'No time like the present.' And so on. Davies's anxiety does not have to be explained; it can be shared. It is familiar. This is just one of many examples of the way in which Pinter draws from the real world in his plays, but heightens common experience through the selection and organisation of his material. He himself has stressed this aspect of his work.

I'm convinced that what happens in my plays could happen anywhere, at any time, in any place, although the events may seem unfamiliar at first glance. If you press me for a definition, I'd say that what goes on in my plays is realistic, but what I'm doing is not realism.
(Introduction to *Pinter Plays: Two*)

Suggestions for further reading

Collections of Pinter's writings (all published as Methuen Paperbacks)

As well as being published individually, all Pinter's plays up to 1981 (except for *The Hothouse*, which is available only in a separate edition) have been collected in four paperback volumes: *Plays: One*, *Plays: Two*, *Plays: Three* and *Plays: Four*. *Other Places* and *One for the Road* are available in separate editions.

Five Screenplays contains *The Servant*, *The Pumpkin Eater*, *The Quiller Memorandum*, *Accident* and *The Go-Between*. *The French Lieutenant's Woman and other screenplays* includes *The Last Tycoon* and *Langrishe, Go Down*. *The Proust Screenplay* is also available.

Poems and Prose 1949–1977 is a selection of Pinter's non-dramatic writings.

Books about Pinter's work

Martin Esslin, *Pinter the Playwright* (Methuen Paperback, 4th revised edition, 1982).

Martin Esslin, *Brief Chronicles — Essays on Modern Theatre* (Temple Smith, 1970). Contains many references to Pinter.

Martin Esslin, *The Theatre of the Absurd* (Penguin, revised 1980). The section on Pinter sets him in a wider, European context.

Ronald Hayman, *Harold Pinter* (Heinemann Educational, Contemporary Playwrights series, 1968).

Charles Marowitz, Tom Milne, Owen Hale (eds.), *New Theatre Voices of the Fifties and Sixties — Selections from Encore Magazine 1956–63* (Methuen Paperback, 1981). Valuable for background to the British theatre at the time of *The Caretaker*.

John Russell Taylor, *Anger and After — A Guide to the New British Drama* (Methuen Paperback, revised 1969). Sections on Pinter and most of his contemporary playwrights.

Simon Trussler, *The Plays of Harold Pinter: An Assessment* (Gollancz, 1973).

Walter Wager (ed.), *The Playwrights Speak* (Longmans, 1969). Includes the *Paris Review* interview with Pinter.

Davies and Aston in the 1962 film.

Aston leaving the house (*above*) and Aston, Mick and Davies fighting for the bag (*below*). Both from the 1962 film.

The Caretaker

This play was first presented by the Arts Theatre Club in association with Michael Codron and David Hall at the Arts Theatre, London, WC2, on 27th April, 1960.

On 30th May, 1960, the play was presented by Michael Codron and David Hall at the Duchess Theatre, London, with the following cast:

MICK, *a man in his late twenties*	Alan Bates
ASTON, *a man in his early thirties*	Peter Woodthorpe
DAVIES, *an old man*	Donald Pleasence

The play was directed by Donald McWhinnie

On 2nd March, 1972, a revival of the play directed by Christopher Morahan was presented at the Mermaid Theatre, London, with the following cast:

MICK	John Hurt
ASTON	Jeremy Kemp
DAVIES	Leonard Rossiter

The action of the play takes place in a house in west London

A room. A window in the back wall, the bottom half covered by a sack. An iron bed along the left wall. Above it a small cupboard, paint buckets, boxes containing nuts, screws, etc. More boxes, vases, by the side of the bed. A door, up right. To the right of the window, a mound: a kitchen sink, a step-ladder, a coal bucket, a lawn-mower, a shopping trolley, boxes, sideboard drawers. Under this mound an iron bed. In front of it a gas stove. On the gas stove a statue of Buddha. Down right, a fireplace. Around it a couple of suitcases, a rolled carpet, a blow-lamp, a wooden chair on its side, boxes, a number of ornaments, a clothes horse, a few short planks of wood, a small electric fire and a very old electric toaster. Below this a pile of old newspapers. Under ASTON'S *bed by the left wall, is an electrolux, which is not seen till used. A bucket hangs from the ceiling.*

Act One

MICK *is alone in the room, sitting on the bed. He wears a leather jacket.*

Silence.

He slowly looks about the room looking at each object in turn. He looks up at the ceiling, and stares at the bucket. Ceasing, he sits quite still, expressionless, looking out front.

Silence for thirty seconds.

A door bangs. Muffled voices are heard.

MICK *turns his head. He stands, moves silently to the door, goes out, and closes the door quietly.*

Silence.

Voices are heard again. They draw nearer, and stop. The door opens. ASTON and DAVIES enter, ASTON first, DAVIES following, shambling, breathing heavily.

ASTON wears an old tweed overcoat, and under it a thin shabby dark-blue pinstripe suit, single-breasted, with a pullover and faded shirt and tie. DAVIES wears a worn brown overcoat, shapeless trousers, a waistcoat, vest, no shirt, and sandals. ASTON puts the key in his pocket and closes the door. DAVIES looks about the room.

ASTON. Sit down.
DAVIES. Thanks. (*Looking about.*) Uuh. . . .
ASTON. Just a minute.

> ASTON *looks around for a chair, sees one lying on its side by the rolled carpet at the fireplace, and starts to get it out.*

DAVIES. Sit down? Huh . . . I haven't had a good·sit down . . . I haven't had a proper sit down . . . well, I couldn't tell you. . . .

ASTON (*placing the chair*). Here you are.

DAVIES. Ten minutes off for a tea-break in the middle of the night in that place and I couldn't find a seat, not one. All them Greeks had it, Poles, Greeks, Blacks, the lot of them, all them aliens had it. And they had me working there . . . they had me working. . . .

> ASTON *sits on the bed, takes out a tobacco tin and papers, and begins to roll himself a cigarette.* DAVIES *watches him.*

All them Blacks had it, Blacks, Greeks, Poles, the lot of them, that's what, doing me out of a seat, treating me like dirt. When he come at me tonight I told him.

> *Pause.*

ASTON. Take a seat.

DAVIES. Yes, but what I got to do first, you see, what I got to do, I got to loosen myself up, you see what I mean? I could have got done in down there.

> DAVIES *exclaims loudly, punches downward with closed fist, turns his back to* ASTON *and stares at the wall.*
> *Pause.* ASTON *lights a cigarette.*

ASTON. You want to roll yourself one of these?

DAVIES (*turning*). What? No, no, I never smoke a cigarette. (*Pause. He comes forward.*) I'll tell you what, though. I'll have a bit of that tobacco there for my pipe, if you like.

ASTON (*handing him the tin*). Yes. Go on. Take some out of that.

DAVIES. That's kind of you, mister. Just enough to fill my pipe, that's all. (*He takes a pipe from his pocket and fills it.*) I had a tin, only . . . only a while ago. But it was knocked off. It was knocked off on the Great West Road. (*He holds out the tin*). Where shall I put it?

ASTON. I'll take it.

DAVIES (*handing the tin*). When he come at me tonight I told him. Didn't I? You heard me tell him, didn't you?

ASTON. I saw him have a go at you.

DAVIES. Go at me? You wouldn't grumble. The filthy skate, an old man like me, I've had dinner with the best.

Pause.

ASTON. Yes, I saw him have a go at you.

DAVIES. All them toe-rags, mate, got the manners of pigs. I might have been on the road a few years but you can take it from me I'm clean. I keep myself up. That's why I left my wife. Fortnight after I married her, no, not so much as that, no more than a week, I took the lid off a saucepan, you know what was in it? A pile of her underclothing, unwashed. The pan for vegetables, it was. The vegetable pan. That's when I left her and I haven't seen her since.

DAVIES turns, shambles across the room, comes face to face with a statue of Buddha standing on the gas stove, looks at it and turns.

I've eaten my dinner off the best of plates. But I'm not young any more. I remember the days I was as handy as any of them. They didn't take any liberties with me. But I haven't been so well lately. I've had a few attacks.

Pause.

(*Coming closer.*) Did you see what happened with that one?

ASTON. I only got the end of it.

DAVIES. Comes up to me, parks a bucket of rubbish at me tells me to take it out the back. It's not my job to take out the bucket! They got a boy there for taking out the bucket. I wasn't engaged to take out buckets. My job's cleaning the floor, clearing up the tables, doing a bit of washing-up, nothing to do with taking out buckets!

ASTON. Uh.

He crosses down right, to get the electric toaster.

DAVIES (*following*). Yes, well say I had! Even if I had! Even if I was supposed to take out the bucket, who was this git to come up and give me orders? We got the same standing. He's not my boss. He's nothing superior to me.

ASTON. What was he, a Greek?

DAVIES. Not him, he was a Scotch. He was a Scotchman. (ASTON *goes back to his bed with the toaster and starts to unscrew the plug.* DAVIES *follows him*). You got an eye of him, did you?

ASTON. Yes.

DAVIES. I told him what to do with his bucket. Didn't I? You heard. Look here, I said, I'm an old man, I said, where I was brought up we had some idea how to talk to old people with the proper respect, we was brought up with the right ideas, if I had a few years off me I'd . . . I'd break you in half. That was after the guvnor give me the bullet. Making too much commotion, he says. Commotion, me! Look here, I said to him, I got my rights. I told him that. I might have been on the road but nobody's got more rights than I have. Let's have a bit of fair play, I said. Anyway, he give me the bullet. (*He sits in the chair*). That's the sort of place.

   Pause.

If you hadn't come out and stopped that Scotch git I'd be inside the hospital now. I'd have cracked my head on that pavement if he'd have landed. I'll get him. One night I'll get him. When I find myself around that direction.

   ASTON *crosses to the plug box to get another plug.*

I wouldn't mind so much but I left all my belongings in that place, in the back room there. All of them, the lot there was, you see, in this bag. Every lousy blasted bit of all my bleeding belongings I left down there now. In the rush of it. I bet he's having a poke around in it now this very moment.

ASTON. I'll pop down sometime and pick them up for you.

   ASTON *goes back to his bed and starts to fix the plug on the toaster.*

DAVIES. Anyway, I'm obliged to you, letting me . . . letting me have a bit of a rest, like . . . for a few minutes. (*He looks about.*) This your room?

ASTON. Yes.

DAVIES. You got a good bit of stuff here.

ASTON. Yes.

DAVIES. Must be worth a few bob, this . . . put it all together.

Pause.

There's enough of it.

ASTON. There's a good bit of it, all right.

DAVIES. You sleep here, do you?

ASTON. Yes.

DAVIES. What, in that?

ASTON. Yes.

DAVIES. Yes, well, you'd be well out of the draught there.

ASTON. You don't get much wind.

DAVIES. You'd be well out of it. It's different when you're kipping out.

ASTON. Would be.

DAVIES. Nothing but wind then.

Pause.

ASTON. Yes, when the wind gets up it. . . .

Pause.

DAVIES. Yes. . . .

ASTON. Mmnn. . . .

Pause.

DAVIES. Gets very draughty.

ASTON. Ah.

DAVIES. I'm very sensitive to it.

ASTON. Are you?

DAVIES. Always have been.

Pause.

You got any more rooms then, have you?

ASTON. Where?

DAVIES. I mean, along the landing here . . . up the landing there.

ASTON. They're out of commission.

DAVIES. Get away.

ASTON. They need a lot of doing to.

Slight pause.

DAVIES. What about downstairs?

ASTON. That's closed up. Needs seeing to. . . . The floors. . . .

Pause.

DAVIES. I was lucky you come into that caff. I might have been done by that Scotch git. I been left for dead more than once.

Pause.

I noticed that there was someone was living in the house next door.

ASTON. What?

DAVIES. (*gesturing*). I noticed. . . .

ASTON. Yes. There's people living all along the road.

DAVIES. Yes, I noticed the curtains pulled down there next door as we came along.

ASTON. They're neighbours.

Pause.

DAVIES. This your house then, is it?

Pause.

ASTON. I'm in charge.

DAVIES. You the landlord, are you?

He puts a pipe in his mouth and puffs without lighting it.

Yes, I noticed them heavy curtains pulled across next door

as we came along. I noticed them heavy big curtains right across the window down there. I thought there must be someone living there.

ASTON. Family of Indians live there.

DAVIES. Blacks?

ASTON. I don't see much of them.

DAVIES. Blacks, eh? (DAVIES *stands and moves about*.) Well you've got some knick-knacks here all right, I'll say that. I don't like a bare room. (ASTON *joins* DAVIES *upstage centre*). I'll tell you what, mate, you haven't got a spare pair of shoes?

ASTON. Shoes?

ASTON *moves downstage right.*

DAVIES. Them bastards at the monastery let me down again.

ASTON. (*going to his bed.*) Where?

DAVIES. Down in Luton. Monastery down at Luton. . . . I got a mate at Shepherd's Bush, you see. . . .

ASTON (*looking under his bed*). I might have a pair.

DAVIES. I got this mate at Shepherd's Bush. In the convenience. Well, he was in the convenience. Run about the best convenience they had. (*He watches* ASTON.) Run about the best one. Always slipped me a bit of soap, any time I went in there. Very good soap. They have to have the best soap. I was never without a piece of soap, whenever I happened to be knocking about the Shepherd's Bush area.

ASTON (*emerging from under the bed with shoes*). Pair of brown.

DAVIES. He's gone now. Went. He was the one who put me on to this monastery. Just the other side of Luton. He'd heard they give away shoes.

ASTON. You've got to have a good pair of shoes.

DAVIES. Shoes? It's life and death to me. I had to go all the way to Luton in these.

ASTON. What happened when you got there, then?

Pause.

DAVIES. I used to know a bootmaker in Acton. He was a good
mate to me.

Pause.

You know what that bastard monk said to me?

Pause.

How many more Blacks you got around here then?

ASTON. What?

DAVIES. You got any more Blacks around here?

ASTON (*holding out the shoes*). See if these are any good.

DAVIES. You know what that bastard monk said to me? (*He
looks over to the shoes.*) I think those'd be a bit small.

ASTON. Would they?

DAVIES. No, don't look the right size.

ASTON. Not bad trim.

DAVIES. Can't wear shoes that don't fit. Nothing worse. I said
to this monk, here, I said, look here, mister, he opened the
door, big door, he opened it, look here, mister, I said, I
come all the way down here, look, I said, I showed him these,
I said, you haven't got a pair of shoes, have you, a pair of
shoes, I said, enough to keep me on my way. Look at these,
they're nearly out, I said, they're no good to me. I heard you
got a stock of shoes here. Piss off, he said to me. Now look
here, I said, I'm an old man, you can't talk to me like that, I
don't care who you are. If you don't piss off, he says, I'll
kick you all the way to the gate. Now look here, I said, now
wait a minute, all I'm asking for is a pair of shoes, you don't
want to start taking liberties with me, it's taken me three
days to get here, I said to him, three days without a bite,
I'm worth a bite to eat, en I? Get out round the corner to
the kitchen, he says, get out round the corner, and when
you've had your meal, piss off out of it. I went round to this
kitchen, see? Meal they give me! A bird, I tell you, a little

bird, a little tiny bird, he could have ate it in under two minutes. Right, they said to me, you've had your meal, get off out of it. Meal? I said, what do you think I am, a dog? Nothing better than a dog. What do you think I am, a wild animal? What about them shoes I come all the way here to get I heard you was giving away? I've a good mind to report you to your mother superior. One of them, an Irish hooligan, come at me. I cleared out. I took a short cut to Watford and picked up a pair there. Got onto the North Circular, just past Hendon, the sole come off, right where I was walking. Lucky I had my old ones wrapped up, still carrying them, otherwise I'd have been finished, man. So I've had to stay with these, you see, they're gone, they're no good, all the good's gone out of them.

ASTON. Try these.

DAVIES *takes the shoes, takes off his sandals and tries them on.*

DAVIES. Not a bad pair of shoes. (*He trudges round the room.*) They're strong, all right. Yes. Not a bad shape of shoe. This leather's hardy, en't? Very hardy. Some bloke tried to flog me some suede the other day. I wouldn't wear them. Can't beat leather, for wear. Suede goes off, it creases, it stains for life in five minutes. You can't beat leather. Yes. Good shoe this.

ASTON. Good.

DAVIES *waggles his feet.*

DAVIES. Don't fit though.

ASTON. Oh?

DAVIES. No. I got a very broad foot.

ASTON. Mmnn.

DAVIES. These are too pointed, you see.

ASTON. Ah.

DAVIES. They'd cripple me in a week. I mean these ones I got on, they're no good but at least they're comfortable. Not much cop, but I mean they don't hurt. (*He takes them off and gives them back*). Thanks anyway, mister.

ASTON. I'll see what I can look out for you.

DAVIES. Good luck. I can't go on like this. Can't get from one place to another. And I'll have to be moving about, you see, try to get fixed up.

ASTON. Where you going to go?

DAVIES. Oh, I got one or two things in mind. I'm waiting for the weather to break.

Pause.

ASTON (*attending to the toaster*). Would . . . would you like to sleep here?

DAVIES. Here?

ASTON. You can sleep here if you like.

DAVIES. Here? Oh, I don't know about that.

Pause.

How long for?

ASTON. Till you . . . get yourself fixed up.

DAVIES (*sitting*). Ay well, that. . . .

ASTON. Get yourself sorted out. . . .

DAVIES. Oh, I'll be fixed up . . . pretty soon now. . . .

Pause.

Where would I sleep?

ASTON. Here. The other rooms would . . . would be no good to you.

DAVIES (*rising, looking about*). Here? Where?

ASTON (*rising, pointing upstage right*). There's a bed behind all that.

DAVIES. Oh, I see. Well, that's handy. Well, that's . . . I tell you what, I might do that . . . just till I get myself sorted out. You got enough furniture here.

ASTON. I picked it up. Just keeping it here for the time being. Thought it might come in handy.

DAVIES. This gas stove work, do it?

ASTON. No.

DAVIES. What do you do for a cup of tea?

ASTON. Nothing.

DAVIES. That's a bit rough. (DAVIES *observes the planks.*) You building something?

ASTON. I might build a shed out the back.

DAVIES. Carpenter, eh? (*He turns to the lawn-mower.*) Got a lawn.

ASTON. Have a look.

ASTON *lifts the sack at the window. They look out.*

DAVIES. Looks a bit thick.

ASTON. Overgrown.

DAVIES. What's that, a pond?

ASTON. Yes.

DAVIES. What you got, fish?

ASTON. No. There isn't anything in there.

Pause.

DAVIES. Where you going to put your shed?

ASTON (*turning*). I'll have to clear the garden first.

DAVIES. You'd need a tractor, man.

ASTON. I'll get it done.

DAVIES. Carpentry, eh?

ASTON (*standing still*). I like . . . working with my hands.

DAVIES *picks up the statue of Buddha.*

DAVIES. What's this?

ASTON (*taking and studying it*). That's a Buddha.

DAVIES. Get on.

ASTON. Yes. I quite like it. Picked it up in a . . . in a shop. Looked quite nice to me. Don't know why. What do you think of these Buddhas?

DAVIES. Oh, they're . . . they're all right, en't they?

ASTON. Yes, I was pleased when I got hold of this one. It's very well made.

DAVIES *turns and peers under the sink.*

DAVIES. This the bed here, is it?

ASTON (*moving to the bed*). We'll get rid of all that. The ladder'll fit under the bed. (*They put the ladder under the bed.*)

DAVIES (*indicating the sink*). What about this?

ASTON. I think that'll fit in under here as well.

DAVIES. I'll give you a hand. (*They lift it.*) It's a ton weight, en't?

ASTON. Under here.

DAVIES. This in use at all, then?

ASTON. No. I'll be getting rid of it. Here.
They place the sink under the bed.
There's a lavatory down the landing. It's got a sink in there. We can put this stuff over there.

They begin to move the coal bucket, shopping trolley, lawn-mower and sideboard drawers to the right wall.

DAVIES (*stopping*). You don't share it, do you?

ASTON. What?

DAVIES. I mean you don't share the toilet with them Blacks, do you?

ASTON. They live next door.

DAVIES. They don't come in?
ASTON puts a drawer against the wall.
Because, you know . . . I mean . . . fair's fair. . . .

ASTON goes to the bed, blows dust and shakes a blanket.

ASTON. You see a blue case?

DAVIES. Blue case? Down here. Look. By the carpet.
ASTON goes to the case, opens it, takes out a sheet and pillow and puts them on the bed.
That's a nice sheet.

ASTON. The blanket'll be a bit dusty.

DAVIES. Don't you worry about that.

> ASTON *stands upright, takes out his tobacco and begins to roll a cigarette. He goes to his bed and sits.*

ASTON. How are you off for money?

DAVIES. Oh well . . . now, mister, if you want the truth . . I'm a bit short.

> ASTON *takes some coins from his pocket, sorts them, and holds out five shillings.*

ASTON. Here's a few bob.

DAVIES (*taking the coins*). Thank you, thank you, good luck. I just happen to find myself a bit short. You see, I got nothing for all that week's work I did last week. That's the position, that's what it is.

> *Pause.*

ASTON. I went into a pub the other day. Ordered a Guinness. They gave it to me in a thick mug. I sat down but I couldn't drink it. I can't drink Guinness from a thick mug. I only like it out of a thin glass. I had a few sips but I couldn't finish it.

> ASTON *picks up a screwdriver and plug from the bed and begins to poke the plug.*

DAVIES (*with great feeling*). If only the weather would break! Then I'd be able to get down to Sidcup!

ASTON. Sidcup?

DAVIES. The weather's so blasted bloody awful, how can I get down to Sidcup in these shoes?

ASTON. Why do you want to get down to Sidcup?

DAVIES. I got my papers there!

> *Pause.*

ASTON. Your what?

DAVIES. I got my papers there!

> *Pause.*

ASTON. What are they doing at Sidcup?

DAVIES. A man I know has got them. I left them with him. You see? They prove who I am! I can't move without them papers. They tell you who I am. You see! I'm stuck without them.

ASTON. Why's that?

DAVIES. You see, what it is, you see, I changed my name! Years ago. I been going around under an assumed name! That's not my real name.

ASTON. What name you been going under?

DAVIES. Jenkins. Bernard Jenkins. That's my name. That's the name I'm known, anyway. But it's no good me going on with that name. I got no rights. I got an insurance card here. (*He takes a card from his pocket.*) Under the name of Jenkins. See? Bernard Jenkins. Look. It's got four stamps on it. Four of them. But I can't go along with these. That's not my real name, they'd find out, they'd have me in the nick. Four stamps. I haven't paid out pennies. I've paid out pounds. I've paid out pounds, not pennies. There's been other stamps, plenty, but they haven't put them on, the nigs, I never had enough time to go into it.

ASTON. They should have stamped your card.

DAVIES. It would have done no good! I'd have got nothing anyway. That's not my real name. If I take that card along I go in the nick.

ASTON. What's your real name, then?

DAVIES. Davies. Mac Davies. That was before I changed my name.

Pause.

ASTON. It looks as though you want to sort all that out.

DAVIES. If only I could get down to Sidcup! I've been waiting for the weather to break. He's got my papers, this man I left them with, it's got it all down there, I could prove everything.

ASTON. How long's he had them?

DAVIES. What?

ASTON. How long's he had them?

DAVIES. Oh, must be . . . it was in the war . . . must be
. . . about near on fifteen year ago.

He suddenly becomes aware of the bucket and looks up.

ASTON. Any time you want to . . . get into bed, just get in.
Don't worry about me.

DAVIES (*taking off his overcoat*). Eh, well, I think I will. I'm a
bit . . . a bit done in. (*He steps out of his trousers, and holds
them out*). Shall I put these on here?

ASTON. Yes.

DAVIES *puts the coat and trousers on the clothes horse.*

DAVIES. I see you got a bucket up here.

ASTON. Leak.

DAVIES *looks up.*

DAVIES. Well, I'll try your bed then. You getting in?

ASTON. I'm mending this plug.

DAVIES *looks at him and then at the gas stove.*

DAVIES. You . . . you can't move this, eh?

ASTON. Bit heavy.

DAVIES. Yes.

DAVIES *gets into bed. He tests his weight and length.*

Not bad. Not bad. A fair bed. I think I'll sleep in this.

ASTON. I'll have to fix a proper shade on that bulb. The
light's a bit glaring.

DAVIES. Don't you worry about that, mister, don't you worry
about that. (*He turns and puts the cover up*).

ASTON *sits, poking his plug.*
The LIGHTS FADE OUT. *Darkness.*
LIGHTS UP. *Morning.*
ASTON *is fastening his trousers, standing by the bed. He
straightens his bed. He turns, goes to the centre of the room*

and looks at DAVIES. *He turns, puts his jacket on, turns, goes towards* DAVIES *and looks down on him.*
He coughs. DAVIES *sits up abruptly.*

DAVIES. What? What's this? What's this?

ASTON. It's all right.

DAVIES (*staring*). What's this?

ASTON. It's all right.

DAVIES *looks about.*

DAVIES. Oh, yes.

ASTON *goes to his bed, picks up the plug and shakes it.*

ASTON. Sleep well?

DAVIES. Yes. Dead out. Must have been dead out.

ASTON *goes downstage right, collects the toaster and examines it.*

ASTON. You . . . er. . . .

DAVIES. Eh?

ASTON. Were you dreaming or something?

DAVIES. Dreaming?

ASTON. Yes.

DAVIES. I don't dream. I've never dreamed.

ASTON. No, nor have I.

DAVIES. Nor me.

Pause.

Why you ask me that, then?

ASTON. You were making noises.

DAVIES. Who was?

ASTON. You were.

DAVIES *gets out of bed. He wears long underpants.*

DAVIES. Now, wait a minute. Wait a minute, what do you mean? What kind of noises?

ASTON. You were making groans. You were jabbering.

DAVIES. Jabbering? Me?

ASTON. Yes.

DAVIES. I don't jabber, man. Nobody ever told me that before.
   Pause.

What would I be jabbering about?

ASTON. I don't know.

DAVIES. I mean, where's the sense in it?
   Pause.

Nobody ever told me that before.
   Pause.

You got hold of the wrong bloke, mate.

ASTON (*crossing to the bed with the toaster*). No. You woke me up. I thought you might have been dreaming.

DAVIES. I wasn't dreaming. I never had a dream in my life.

   Pause.

ASTON. Maybe it was the bed.

DAVIES. Nothing wrong with this bed.

ASTON. Might be a bit unfamiliar.

DAVIES. There's nothing unfamiliar about me with beds. I slept in beds. I don't make noises just because I sleep in a bed. I slept in plenty of beds.
   Pause.

I tell you what, maybe it were them Blacks.

ASTON. What?

DAVIES. Them noises.

ASTON. What Blacks?

DAVIES. Them you got. Next door. Maybe it were them Blacks making noises, coming up through the walls.

ASTON. Hmmnn.

DAVIES. That's my opinion.

   ASTON *puts down the plug and moves to the door.*

Where you going, you going out?

ASTON. Yes.

DAVIES (*seizing the sandals*). Wait a minute then, just a minute.

ASTON. What you doing?

DAVIES (*putting on the sandals*). I better come with you.

ASTON. Why?

DAVIES. I mean, I better come out with you, anyway.

ASTON. Why?

DAVIES. Well . . . don't you want me to go out?

ASTON. What for?

DAVIES. I mean . . . when you're out. Don't you want me to get out . . . when you're out?

ASTON. You don't have to go out.

DAVIES. You mean . . . I can stay here?

ASTON. Do what you like. You don't have to come out just because I go out.

DAVIES. You don't mind me staying here?

ASTON. I've got a couple of keys. (*He goes to a box by his bed and finds them.*) This door and the front door. (*He hands them to* DAVIES.)

DAVIES. Thanks very much, the best of luck.

Pause. ASTON *stands.*

ASTON. I think I'll take a stroll down the road. A little . . . kind of a shop. Man there'd got a jig saw the other day. I quite liked the look of it.

DAVIES. A jig saw, mate?

ASTON. Yes. Could be very useful.

DAVIES. Yes.

Slight pause.

What's that then, exactly, then?

ASTON *walks up to the window and looks out.*

ASTON. A jig saw? Well, it comes from the same family as the fret saw. But it's an appliance, you see. You have to fix it on to a portable drill.

DAVIES. Ah, that's right. They're very handy.

ASTON. They are, yes.

Pause.

You know, I was sitting in a café the other day. I happened to be sitting at the same table as this woman. Well, we

started to . . . we started to pick up a bit of a conversation.
I don't know . . . about her holiday, it was, where she'd
been. She'd been down to the south coast. I can't remember
where though. Anyway, we were just sitting there, having
this bit of a conversation . . . then suddenly she put her
hand over to mine . . . and she said, how would you like
me to have a look at your body?

DAVIES. Get out of it.

Pause.

ASTON. Yes. To come out with it just like that, in the middle
of this conversation. Struck me as a bit odd.

DAVIES. They've said the same thing to me.

ASTON. Have they?

DAVIES. Women? There's many a time they've come up to
me and asked me more or less the same question.

Pause.

ASTON. What did you say your name was?

DAVIES. Bernard Jenkins is my assumed one.

ASTON. No, your other one?

DAVIES. Davies. Mac Davies.

ASTON. Welsh, are you?

DAVIES. Eh?

ASTON. You Welsh?

Pause.

DAVIES. Well, I been around, you know . . . what I mean
. . . I been about. . . .

ASTON. Where were you born then?

DAVIES. (*darkly*). What do you mean?

ASTON. Where were you born?

DAVIES. I was . . . uh . . . oh, it's a bit hard, like, to set
your mind back . . . see what I mean . . . going back
. . . . a good way . . . lose a bit of track, like . . . you
know. . . .

ASTON (*going to below the fireplace*). See this plug? Switch it on here, if you like. This little fire.

DAVIES. Right, mister.

ASTON. Just plug in here.

DAVIES. Right, mister.

 ASTON *goes towards the door.*

(*Anxiously*). What do I do?

ASTON. Just switch it on, that's all. The fire'll come on.

DAVIES. I tell you what. I won't bother about it.

ASTON. No trouble.

DAVIES. No, I don't go in for them things much.

ASTON. Should work. (*Turning*). Right.

DAVIES. Eh, I was going to ask you, mister, what about this stove? I mean, do you think it's going to be letting out any . . . what do you think?

ASTON. It's not connected.

DAVIES. You see, the trouble is, it's right on top of my bed, you see? What I got to watch is nudging . . . one of them gas taps with my elbow when I get up, you get my meaning?

He goes round to the other side of stove and examines it.

ASTON. There's nothing to worry about.

DAVIES. Now look here, don't you worry about it. All I'll do, I'll keep an eye on these taps every now and again, like, you see. See they're switched off. You leave it to me.

ASTON. I don't think . . . .

DAVIES (*coming round*). Eh, mister, just one thing . . . eh . . . . you couldn't slip me a couple of bob, for a cup of tea, just, you know?

ASTON. I gave you a few bob last night.

DAVIES. Eh, so you did. So you did. I forgot. Went clean out of my mind. That's right. Thank you, mister. Listen. You're sure now, you're sure you don't mind me staying here? I mean, I'm not the sort of man who wants to take any liberties.

ASTON. No, that's all right.

DAVIES. I might get down to Wembley later on in the day.

ASTON. Uh-uh.

DAVIES. There's a caff down there, you see, might be able to get fixed up there. I was there, see? I know they were a bit short-handed. They might be in the need of a bit of staff.

ASTON. When was that?

DAVIES. Eh? Oh, well, that was . . . near on . . . that'll be . . . that'll be a little while ago now. But of course what it is, they can't find the right kind of people in these places. What they want to do, they're trying to do away with these foreigners, you see, in catering. They want an Englishman to pour their tea, that's what they want, that's what they're crying out for. It's only common sense, en't? Oh, I got all that under way . . . that's . . . uh . . . that's . . . what I'll be doing.

Pause.

If only I could get down there.

ASTON. Mmnn. (ASTON *moves to the door.*) Well, I'll be seeing you then.

DAVIES. Yes. Right.

ASTON *goes out and closes the door.*

DAVIES *stands still. He waits a few seconds, then goes to the door, opens it, looks out, closes it, stands with his back to it, turns swiftly, opens it, looks out, comes back, closes the door, finds the keys in his pocket, tries one, tries the other, locks the door. He looks about the room. He then goes quickly to* ASTON'S *bed, bends, brings out the pair of shoes and examines them.*

Not a bad pair of shoes. Bit pointed.

He puts them back under the bed. He examines the area by ASTON'S *bed, picks up a vase and looks into it, then picks up a box and shakes it.*

Screws!

He sees paint buckets at the top of the bed, goes to them, and examines them.

Paint. What's he going to paint?

He puts the bucket down, comes to the centre of the room, looks up at bucket, and grimaces.

I'll have to find out about that. (*He crosses right, and picks up a blow-lamp.*) He's got some stuff in here. (*He picks up the Buddha and looks at it.*) Full of stuff. Look at all this. (*His eye falls on the piles of papers.*) What's he got all those papers for? Damn pile of papers.

He goes to a pile and touches it. The pile wobbles. He steadies it.

Hold it, hold it!

He holds the pile and pushes the papers back into place. The door opens.

MICK *comes in, puts the key in his pocket, and closes the door silently. He stands at the door and watches* DAVIES.

What's he got all these papers for? (DAVIES *climbs over the rolled carpet to the blue case.*) Had a sheet and pillow ready in here. (*He opens the case.*) Nothing. (*He shuts the case.*) Still, I had a sleep though. I don't make no noises. (*He looks at the window.*) What's this?

He picks up another case and tries to open it. MICK *moves upstage, silently.*

Locked. (*He puts it down and moves downstage.*) Must be something in it. (*He picks up a sideboard drawer, rummages in the contents, then puts it down.*)

MICK *slides across the room.*

DAVIES *half turns,* MICK *seizes his arm and forces it up his back.* DAVIES *screams.*

Uuuuuuuhhh! Uuuuuuuhhh! What! What! What! Uuuuuuuhhh!

MICK *swiftly forces him to the floor, with* DAVIES *struggling, grimacing, whimpering and staring.*

MICK *holds his arm, puts his other hand to his lips, then puts his hand to* DAVIES' *lips.* DAVIES *quietens.* MICK *lets him go.* DAVIES *writhes.* MICK *holds out a warning finger. He then squats down to regard* DAVIES. *He regards him, then stands looking down on him.* DAVIES *massages his arm, watching* MICK. MICK *turns slowly to look at the room. He goes to* DAVIES' *bed and uncovers it. He turns, goes to the clothes horse and picks up* DAVIES' *trousers.* DAVIES *starts to rise.* MICK *presses him down with his foot and stands over him. Finally he removes his foot. He examines the trousers and throws them back.* DAVIES *remains on the floor, crouched.* MICK *slowly goes to the chair, sits, and watches* DAVIES, *expressionless.*

Silence.

MICK. What's the game?

Curtain.

Act Two

A few seconds later.

> MICK *is seated*, DAVIES *on the floor, half seated, crouched.*
> *Silence.*

MICK. Well?

DAVIES. Nothing, nothing. Nothing.

> *A drip sounds in the bucket overhead. They look up.* MICK
> *looks back to* DAVIES.

MICK. What's your name?

DAVIES. I don't know you. I don't know who you are.

> *Pause.*

MICK. Eh?

DAVIES. Jenkins.

MICK. Jenkins?

DAVIES. Yes.

MICK. Jen . . . kins.

> *Pause.*

You sleep here last night?

DAVIES. Yes.

MICK. Sleep well?

DAVIES. Yes.

MICK. I'm awfully glad. It's awfully nice to meet you.

> *Pause.*

What did you say your name was?

DAVIES. Jenkins.

MICK. I beg your pardon?

DAVIES. Jenkins!

> *Pause.*

MICK. Jen . . . kins.

A drip sounds in the bucket. DAVIES *looks up.*

You remind me of my uncle's brother. He was always on the move, that man. Never without his passport. Had an eye for the girls. Very much your build. Bit of an athlete. Long-jump specialist. He had a habit of demonstrating different run-ups in the drawing-room round about Christmas time. Had a penchant for nuts. That's what it was. Nothing else but a penchant. Couldn't eat enough of them. Peanuts, walnuts, brazil nuts, monkey nuts, wouldn't touch a piece of fruit cake. Had a marvellous stop-watch. Picked it up in Hong Kong. The day after they chucked him out of the Salvation Army. Used to go in number four for Beckenham Reserves. That was before he got his Gold Medal. Had a funny habit of carrying his fiddle on his back. Like a papoose. I think there was a bit of the Red Indian in him. To be honest, I've never made out how he came to be my uncle's brother. I've often thought that maybe it was the other way round. I mean that my uncle was his brother and he was my uncle. But I never called him uncle. As a matter of fact I called him Sid. My mother called him Sid too. It was a funny business. Your spitting image he was. Married a Chinaman and went to Jamaica.

Pause.

I hope you slept well last night.

DAVIES. Listen! I don't know who you are!

MICK. What bed you sleep in?

DAVIES. Now look here—

MICK. Eh?

DAVIES. That one.

MICK. Not the other one?

DAVIES. No.

MICK. Choosy.

Pause.

How do you like my room?

DAVIES. Your room?

MICK. Yes.

DAVIES. This ain't your room. I don't know who you are. I ain't never seen you before.

MICK. You know, believe it or not, you've got a funny kind of resemblance to a bloke I once knew in Shoreditch. Actually he lived in Aldgate. I was staying with a cousin in Camden Town. This chap, he used to have a pitch in Finsbury Park, just by the bus depot. When I got to know him I found out he was brought up in Putney. That didn't make any difference to me. I know quite a few people who were born in Putney. Even if they weren't born in Putney they were born in Fulham. The only trouble was, he wasn't born in Putney, he was only brought up in Putney. It turned out he was born in the Caledonian Road, just before you get to the Nag's Head. His old mum was still living at the Angel. All the buses passed right by the door. She could get a 38, 581, 30 or 38A, take her down the Essex Road to Dalston Junction in next to no time. Well, of course, if she got the 30 he'd take her up Upper Street way, round by Highbury Corner and down to St. Paul's Church, but she'd get to Dalston Junction just the same in the end. I used to leave my bike in her garden on my way to work. Yes, it was a curious affair. Dead spit of you he was. Bit bigger round the nose but there was nothing in it.

Pause.

Did you sleep here last night?

DAVIES. Yes.

MICK. Sleep well?

DAVIES. Yes!

MICK. Did you have to get up in the night?

DAVIES. No!

Pause.

MICK. What's your name?

DAVIES (*shifting, about to rise*). Now look here!

MICK. What?

DAVIES. Jenkins!

MICK. Jen . . . kins.

> DAVIES *makes a sudden move to rise. A violent bellow from* MICK *sends him back.*

(*A shout.*) Sleep here last night?

DAVIES. Yes. . . .

MICK (*continuing at great pace*). How'd you sleep?

DAVIES. I slept—

MICK. Sleep well?

DAVIES. Now look—

MICK. What bed?

DAVIES. That—

MICK. Not the other?

DAVIES. No!

MICK. Choosy.

> *Pause.*

(*Quietly.*) Choosy.

> *Pause.*

(*Again amiable.*) What sort of sleep did you have in that bed?

DAVIES (*banging on floor*). All right!

MICK. You weren't uncomfortable?

DAVIES (*groaning*). All right!

> MICK *stands, and moves to him.*

MICK. You a foreigner?

DAVIES. No.

MICK. Born and bred in the British Isles?

DAVIES. I was!

MICK. What did they teach you?

> *Pause.*

How did you like my bed?

> *Pause.*

That's my bed. You want to mind you don't catch a draught.

DAVIES. From the bed?

MICK. No, now, up your arse.

> DAVIES *stares warily at* MICK, *who turns.* DAVIES
> *scrambles to the clothes horse and seizes his trousers.* MICK
> *turns swiftly and grabs them.* DAVIES *lunges for them.*
> MICK *holds out a hand warningly.*

You intending to settle down here?

DAVIES. Give me my trousers then.

MICK. You settling down for a long stay?

DAVIES. Give me my bloody trousers!

MICK. Why, where you going?

DAVIES. Give me and I'm going, I'm going to Sidcup!

> MICK *flicks the trousers in* DAVIES' *face several times.*
> DAVIES *retreats.*
> *Pause.*

MICK. You know, you remind me of a bloke I bumped into
once, just the other side of the Guildford by-pass—

DAVIES. I was brought here!

> *Pause.*

MICK. Pardon?

DAVIES. I was brought here! I was brought here!

MICK. Brought here? Who brought you here?

DAVIES. Man who lives here . . . he. . . .

> *Pause.*

MICK. Fibber.

DAVIES. I was brought here, last night . . . met him in a
caff . . . I was working . . . I got the bullet . . . I was
working there . . . bloke saved me from a punch up,
brought me here, brought me right here.

> *Pause.*

MICK. I'm afraid you're a born fibber, en't you? You're
speaking to the owner. This is my room. You're standing
in my house.

DAVIES. It's his . . . he seen me all right . . . he. . . .

MICK (*pointing to* DAVIES' *bed*). That's my bed.

DAVIES. What about that, then?

MICK. That's my mother's bed.

DAVIES. Well she wasn't in it last night!

MICK (*moving to him*). Now don't get perky, son, don't get perky. Keep your hands off my old mum.

DAVIES. I ain't . . . I haven't. . . .

MICK. Don't get out of your depth, friend, don't start taking liberties with my old mother, let's have a bit of respect.

DAVIES. I got respect, you won't find anyone with more respect.

MICK. Well, stop telling me all these fibs.

DAVIES. Now listen to me, I never seen you before, have I?

MICK. Never seen my mother before either, I suppose?

Pause.

I think I'm coming to the conclusion that you're an old rogue. You're nothing but an old scoundrel.

DAVIES. Now wait—

MICK. Listen, son. Listen, sonny. You stink.

DAVIES. You ain't got no right to—

MICK. You're stinking the place out. You're an old robber, there's no getting away from it. You're an old skate. You don't belong in a nice place like this. You're an old barbarian. Honest. You got no business wandering about in an unfurnished flat. I could charge seven quid a week for this if I wanted to. Get a taker tomorrow. Three hundred and fifty a year exclusive. No argument. I mean, if that sort of money's in your range don't be afraid to say so. Here you are. Furniture and fittings, I'll take four hundred or the nearest offer. Rateable value ninety quid for the annum. You can reckon water, heating and lighting at close on fifty. That'll cost you eight hundred and ninety if you're all that keen. Say the word and I'll have my solicitors draft you out a contract. Otherwise I've got the van outside, I can run you to the police station in five minutes, have you in for trespassing, loitering with intent, daylight robbery, filching, thieving and stinking the place out. What do you say? Unless you're really keen on a straightforward purchase. Of course, I'll get my brother to decorate it up for you first. I've got a brother who's a number one decorator. He'll decorate it up for you. If you want more space, there's four more rooms along the landing ready to go. Bathroom, living-room, bedroom and nursery. You can have this as your study. This brother I mentioned, he's just about to start on the other rooms. Yes, just about to start. So what do you say? Eight hundred odd for this room or three thousand down for the whole upper storey. On the other hand, if you prefer to approach it in the long-term way I know an insurance firm in West Ham'll be pleased to handle the deal for you. No strings attached, open and above board, untarnished record; twenty per cent interest, fifty per cent deposit; down payments, back payments, family allowances, bonus schemes, remission of term for good behaviour, six months lease, yearly examination of the relevant archives, tea laid on, disposal of shares, benefit extension, compensation on cessation, comprehensive indemnity against Riot, Civil Commotion, Labour Disturbances, Storm, Tempest, Thunderbolt, Larceny or Cattle all subject to a daily check and double check. Of course we'd need a signed declaration from your personal medical attendant as assurance that you possess the requisite fitness to carry the can, won't we? Who do you bank with?

Pause.

Who do you bank with?

The door opens. ASTON *comes in.* MICK *turns and drops the trousers.* DAVIES *picks them up and puts them on.* ASTON, *after a glance at the other two, goes to his bed, places a bag which he is carrying on it, sits down and resumes fixing the toaster.* DAVIES *retreats to his corner.* MICK *sits in the chair.*

Silence.
A drip sounds in the bucket. They all look up.
Silence.

You still got that leak.

ASTON. Yes.

Pause.

It's coming from the roof.

MICK. From the roof, eh?

ASTON. Yes.

Pause.

I'll have to tar it over.

MICK. You're going to tar it over?

ASTON. Yes.

MICK. What?

ASTON. The cracks.

Pause.

MICK. You'll be tarring over the cracks on the roof.

ASTON. Yes.

Pause.

MICK. Think that'll do it?

ASTON. It'll do it, for the time being.

MICK. Uh.

Pause.

DAVIES (*abruptly*). What do you do—?
    They both look at him.
What do you do . . . when that bucket's full?

Pause.

ASTON. Empty it.

Pause.

MICK. I was telling my friend you were about to start decorating the other rooms.

ASTON. Yes.

  Pause.

  (*To* DAVIES.) I got your bag.

DAVIES. Oh. (*Crossing to him and taking it*). Oh thanks, mister, thanks. Give it to you, did they?

  DAVIES *crosses back with the bag.*
  MICK *rises and snatches it.*

MICK. What's this?

DAVIES. Give us it, that's my bag!

MICK (*warding him off*). I've seen this bag before.

DAVIES. That's my bag!

MICK (*eluding him*). This bag's very familiar.

DAVIES. What do you mean?

MICK. Where'd you get it?

ASTON (*rising, to them*). Scrub it.

DAVIES. That's mine.

MICK. Whose?

DAVIES. It's mine! Tell him it's mine!

MICK. This your bag?

DAVIES. Give me it!

ASTON. Give it to him.

MICK. What? Give him what?

DAVIES. That bloody bag!

MICK (*slipping it behind the gas stove*). What bag? (*To* DAVIES.) What bag?

DAVIES (*moving*). Look here!

MICK (*facing him*). Where you going?

DAVIES. I'm going to get . . . my old . . .

MICK. Watch your step, sonny! You're knocking at the door when no one's at home. Don't push it too hard. You come busting into a private house, laying your hands on anything you can lay your hands on. Don't overstep the mark, son.

  ASTON *picks up the bag.*

DAVIES. You thieving bastard ... you thieving skate ...
let me get my—
ASTON. Here you are. (ASTON *offers the bag to* DAVIES.)

    MICK *grabs it.* ASTON *takes it.*

    MICK *grabs it.* DAVIES *reaches for it.*

    ASTON *takes it.* MICK *reaches for it.*

    ASTON *gives it to* DAVIES. MICK *grabs it.*

    Pause.

    ASTON *takes it.* DAVIES *takes it.* MICK *takes it.* DAVIES
    reaches for it. ASTON *takes it.*

    Pause.

    ASTON *gives it to* MICK. MICK *gives it to* DAVIES.

    DAVIES *grasps it to him.*

    Pause.

    MICK *looks at* ASTON. DAVIES *moves away with the bag.*
    He drops it.

    Pause.

    They watch him. He picks it up. Goes to his bed, and sits.
    ASTON *goes to his bed, sits, and begins to roll a cigarette.*
    MICK *stands still.*

    Pause.

    A drip sounds in the bucket. They all look up.

    Pause.

How did you get on at Wembley?
DAVIES. Well, I didn't get down there.

    Pause.

No. I couldn't make it.

    MICK *goes to the door and exits.*

ASTON. I had a bit of bad luck with that jig saw. When I got
there it had gone.

    Pause.

DAVIES. Who was that feller?
ASTON. He's my brother.
DAVIES. Is he? He's a bit of a joker, en'he?

ASTON. Uh.

DAVIES. Yes . . . he's a real joker.

ASTON. He's got a sense of humour.

DAVIES. Yes, I noticed.

> *Pause.*

He's a real joker, that lad, you can see that.

> *Pause.*

ASTON. Yes, he tends . . . he tends to see the funny side of things.

DAVIES. Well, he's got a sense of humour, en' he?

ASTON. Yes.

DAVIES. Yes, you could tell that.

> *Pause.*

I could tell the first time I saw him he had his own way of looking at things.

> ASTON *stands, goes to the sideboard drawer, right, picks up the statue of Buddha, and puts it on the gas stove.*

ASTON. I'm supposed to be doing up the upper part of the house for him.

DAVIES. What . . . you mean . . . you mean it's his house?

ASTON. Yes. I'm supposed to be decorating this landing for him. Make a flat out of it.

DAVIES. What does he do, then?

ASTON. He's in the building trade. He's got his own van.

DAVIES. He don't live here, do he?

ASTON. Once I get that shed up outside . . . I'll be able to give a bit more thought to the flat, you see. Perhaps I can knock up one or two things for it. (*He walks to the window.*) I can work with my hands, you see. That's one thing I can do. I never knew I could. But I can do all sorts of things now, with my hands. You know, manual things. When I get that shed up out there . . . I'll have a workshop, you see. I . . . could do a bit of woodwork. Simple woodwork, to start. Working with . . . good wood.

Pause.

Of course, there's a lot to be done to this place. What I think, though, I think I'll put in a partition ... in one of the rooms along the landing. I think it'll take it. You know ... they've got these screens ... you know ... Oriental. They break up a room with them. Make it into two parts. I could either do that or I could have a partition. I could knock them up, you see, if I had a workshop.

Pause.

Anyway, I think I've decided on the partition.

Pause.

DAVIES. Eh, look here, I been thinking. This ain't my bag.

ASTON. Oh. No.

DAVIES. No, this ain't my bag. My bag, it was another kind of bag altogether, you see. I know what they've done. What they done, they kept my bag, and they given you another one altogether.

ASTON. No ... what happened was, someone had gone off with your bag.

DAVIES (*rising*). That's what I said!

ASTON. Anyway, I picked that bag up somewhere else. It's got a few ... pieces of clothes in it too. He let me have the whole lot cheap.

DAVIES (*opening the bag*). Any shoes?

DAVIES *takes two check shirts, bright red and bright green, from the bag. He holds them up.*

Check.

ASTON. Yes.

DAVIES. Yes ... well, I know about these sort of shirts, you see. Shirts like these, they don't go far in the winter-time. I mean, that's one thing I know for a fact. No, what I need, is a kind of a shirt with stripes, a good solid shirt, with stripes going down. That's what I want. (*He takes from the bag a deep-red velvet smoking-jacket.*) What's this?

ASTON. It's a smoking-jacket.

DAVIES. A smoking-jacket? (*He feels it.*) This ain't a bad piece of cloth. I'll see how it fits.

> *He tries it on.*

You ain't got a mirror here, have you?

ASTON. I don't think I have.

DAVIES. Well, it don't fit too bad. How do you think it looks?

ASTON. Looks all right.

DAVIES. Well, I won't say no to this, then.

> ASTON *picks up the plug and examines it.*

No, I wouldn't say no to this.

> *Pause.*

ASTON. You could be . . . caretaker here, if you liked.

DAVIES. What?

ASTON. You could . . . look after the place, if you liked . . . you know, the stairs and the landing, the front steps, keep an eye on it. Polish the bells.

DAVIES. Bells?

ASTON. I'll be fixing a few, down by the front door. Brass.

DAVIES. Caretaking, eh?

ASTON. Yes.

DAVIES. Well, I . . . I never done caretaking before, you know . . . I mean to say . . . I never . . . what I mean to say is . . . I never been a caretaker before.

> *Pause.*

ASTON. How do you feel about being one, then?

DAVIES. Well, I reckon . . . Well, I'd have to know . . . you know. . . .

ASTON. What sort of. . . .

DAVIES. Yes, what sort of . . . you know. . . .

> *Pause.*

ASTON. Well, I mean. . . .

DAVIES. I mean, I'd have to . . . I'd have to. . . .

ASTON. Well, I could tell you. . . .

DAVIES. That's . . . that's it . . . you see . . . you get my
meaning?

ASTON. When the time comes. . . .

DAVIES. I mean, that's what I'm getting at, you see. . . .

ASTON. More or less exactly what you. . . .

DAVIES. You see, what I mean to say . . . what I'm getting
at is . . . I mean, what sort of jobs. . . .

Pause.

ASTON. Well, there's things like the stairs . . . and the . . .
the bells. . . .

DAVIES. But it'd be a matter . . . wouldn't it . . . it'd be a
matter of a broom . . . isn't it?

ASTON. Yes, and of course, you'd need a few brushes.

DAVIES. You'd need implements . . . you see . . . you'd
need a good few implements. . . .

ASTON *takes a white overall from a nail over his bed, and
shows it to* DAVIES.

ASTON. You could wear this, if you liked.

DAVIES. Well . . . that's nice, en't?

ASTON. It'd keep the dust off.

DAVIES (*putting it on*). Yes, this'd keep the dust off, all right.
Well off. Thanks very much, mister.

ASTON. You see, what we could do, we could . . . I could fit
a bell at the bottom, outside the front door, with "Caretaker"
on it. And you could answer any queries.

DAVIES. Oh, I don't know about that.

ASTON. Why not?

DAVIES. Well, I mean, you don't know who might come up
them front steps, do you? I got to be a bit careful.

ASTON. Why, someone after you?

DAVIES. After me? Well, I could have that Scotch git coming
looking after me, couldn't I? All I'd do, I'd hear the bell, I'd
go down there, open the door, who might be there, any Harry

might be there. I could be buggered as easy as that, man. They might be there after my card, I mean look at it, here I am, I only got four stamps, on this card, here it is, look, four stamps, that's all I got, I ain't got any more, that's all I got, they ring the bell called Caretaker, they'd have me in, that's what they'd do, I wouldn't stand a chance. Of course I got plenty of other cards lying about, but they don't know that, and I can't tell them, can I, because then they'd find out I was going about under an assumed name. You see, the name I call myself now, that's not my real name. My real name's not the one I'm using, you see. It's different. You see, the name I go under now ain't my real one. It's assumed.

Silence.
THE LIGHTS FADE TO BLACKOUT.
THEN UP TO DIM LIGHT THROUGH THE WINDOW.
A door bangs.
Sound of a key in the door of the room.
DAVIES *enters, closes the door, and tries the light switch, on, off, on, off.*

DAVIES (*muttering*). What's this? (*He switches on and off.*) What's the matter with this damn light? (*He switches on and off.*) Aaah. Don't tell me the damn light's gone now.
  Pause.
What'll I do? Damn light's gone now. Can't see a thing.
  Pause.
What'll I do now? (*He moves, stumbles.*) Ah God, what's that? Give me a light. Wait a minute.
  He feels for matches in his pocket, takes out a box and lights one. The match goes out. The box falls.
Aah! Where is it? (*Stooping.*) Where's the bloody box?
  The box is kicked.
What's that? What? Who's that? What's that?
  Pause. He moves.

Where's my box? It was down here. Who's this? Who's moving it?

Silence.

Come on. Who's this? Who's this got my box?

Pause.

Who's in here!

Pause.

I got a knife here. I'm ready. Come on then, who are you?

He moves, stumbles, falls and cries out.

Silence.

A faint whimper from DAVIES. *He gets up.*

All right!

He stands. Heavy breathing.

Suddenly the electrolux starts to hum. A figure moves with it, guiding it. The nozzle moves along the floor after DAVIES, *who skips, dives away from it and falls, breathlessly.*

Ah, ah, ah, ah, ah, ah! Get away-y-y-y-y!

The electrolux stops. The figure jumps on ASTON'S *bed.*

I'm ready for you! I'm . . . I'm . . . I'm here!

The figure takes out the electrolux plug from the light socket and fits the bulb. The light goes on. DAVIES *flattens himself against right wall, knife in hand.* MICK *stands on the bed, holding the plug.*

MICK. I was just doing some spring cleaning. (*He gets down.*) There used to be a wall plug for this electrolux. But it doesn't work. I had to fit it in the light socket. (*He puts the electrolux under* ASTON'S *bed.*) How do you think the place is looking? I gave it a good going over.

Pause.

We take it in turns, once a fortnight, my brother and me, to give the place a thorough going over. I was working late to-night, I only just got here. But I thought I better get on with it, as it's my turn.

Pause.

It's not that I actually live here. I don't. As a matter of fact I live somewhere else. But after all, I'm responsible for the upkeep of the premises, en' I? Can't help being house-proud.

He moves towards DAVIES *and indicates the knife.*

What are you waving that about for?

DAVIES. You come near me. . . .

MICK. I'm sorry if I gave you a start. But I had you in mind too, you know. I mean, my brother's guest. We got to think of your comfort, en't we? Don't want the dust to get up your nose. How long you thinking of staying here, by the way? As a matter of fact, I was going to suggest that we'd lower your rent, make it just a nominal sum, I mean until you get fixed up. Just nominal, that's all.

Pause.

Still, if you're going to be spiky, I'll have to reconsider the whole proposition.

Pause.

Eh, you're not thinking of doing any violence on me, are you? You're not the violent sort, are you?

DAVIES (*vehemently*). I keep myself to myself, mate. But if anyone starts with me though, they know what they got coming.

MICK. I can believe that.

DAVIES. You do. I been all over, see? You understand my meaning? I don't mind a bit of a joke now and then, but anyone'll tell you . . . that no one starts anything with me.

MICK. I get what you mean, yes.

DAVIES. I can be pushed so far . . . but. . . .

MICK. No further.

DAVIES. That's it.

MICK *sits on junk down right.*

What you doing?

MICK. No, I just want to say that . . . I'm very impressed
by that.

DAVIES. Eh?

MICK. I'm very impressed by what you've just said.

Pause.

Yes, that's impressive, that is.

Pause.

I'm impressed, anyway.

DAVIES. You know what I'm talking about then?

MICK. Yes, I know. I think we understand one another.

DAVIES. Uh? Well . . . I'll tell you . . . I'd . . . I'd like
to think that. You been playing me about, you know. I don't
know why. I never done you no harm.

MICK. No, you know what it was? We just got off on the wrong
foot. That's all it was.

DAVIES. Ay, we did.

DAVIES *joins* MICK *in junk.*

MICK. Like a sandwich?

DAVIES. What?

MICK (*taking a sandwich from his pocket*). Have one of these.

DAVIES. Don't you pull anything.

MICK. No, you're still not understanding me. I can't help
being interested in any friend of my brother's. I mean,
you're my brother's friend, aren't you?

DAVIES. Well, I . . . I wouldn't put it as far as that.

MICK. Don't you find him friendly, then?

DAVIES. Well, I wouldn't say we was all that friends. I mean,
he done me no harm, but I wouldn't say he was any particular friend of mine. What's in that sandwich, then?

MICK. Cheese.

DAVIES. That'll do me.

MICK. Take one.

DAVIES. Thank you, mister.

MICK. I'm sorry to hear my brother's not very friendly.

DAVIES. He's friendly, he's friendly, I didn't say he wasn't. . . .

MICK (*taking a salt-cellar from his pocket*). Salt?

DAVIES. No thanks. (*He munches the sandwich.*) I just can't exactly . . . make him out.

MICK (*feeling in his pocket*). I forgot the pepper.

DAVIES. Just can't get the hang of him, that's all.

MICK. I had a bit of beetroot somewhere. Must have mislaid it.

> Pause.

> DAVIES *chews the sandwich.* MICK *watches him eat. He then rises and strolls downstage.*

Uuh . . . listen . . . can I ask your advice? I mean, you're a man of the world. Can I ask your advice about something?

DAVIES. You go right ahead.

MICK. Well, what it is, you see, I'm . . . I'm a bit worried about my brother.

DAVIES. Your brother?

MICK. Yes . . . you see, his trouble is. . . .

DAVIES. What?

MICK. Well, it's not a very nice thing to say. . . .

DAVIES (*rising, coming downstage*). Go on now, you say it.

> MICK *looks at him.*

MICK. He doesn't like work.

> Pause.

DAVIES. Go on!

MICK. No, he just doesn't like work, that's his trouble.

DAVIES. Is that a fact?

MICK. It's a terrible thing to have to say about your own brother.

DAVIES. Ay.

MICK. He's just shy of it. Very shy of it.

DAVIES. I know that sort.

MICK. You know the type?

DAVIES. I've met them.

MICK. I mean, I want to get him going in the world.

DAVIES. Stands to reason, man.

MICK. If you got an older brother you want to push him on, you want to see him make his way. Can't have him idle, he's only doing himself harm. That's what I say.

DAVIES. Yes.

MICK. But he won't buckle down to the job.

DAVIES. He don't like work.

MICK. Work shy.

DAVIES. Sounds like it to me.

MICK. You've met the type, have you?

DAVIES. Me? I know that sort.

MICK. Yes.

DAVIES. I know that sort. I've met them.

MICK. Causing me great anxiety. You see, I'm a working man: I'm a tradesman. I've got my own van.

DAVIES. Is that a fact?

MICK. He's supposed to be doing a little job for me . . . I keep him here to do a little job . . . but I don't know . . . I'm coming to the conclusion he's a slow worker.

Pause.

What would your advice be?

DAVIES. Well . . . he's a funny bloke, your brother.

MICK. What?

DAVIES. I was saying, he's . . . he's a bit of a funny bloke, your brother.

MICK *stares at him.*

MICK. Funny? Why?

DAVIES. Well . . . he's funny. . . .

MICK. What's funny about him?

Pause.

DAVIES. Not liking work.

MICK. What's funny about that?

DAVIES. Nothing.

Pause.

MICK. I don't call it funny.

DAVIES. Nor me.

MICK. You don't want to start getting hypercritical.

DAVIES. No, no, I wasn't that, I wasn't . . . I was only saying. . . .

MICK. Don't get too glib.

DAVIES. Look, all I meant was—

MICK. Cut it! (*Briskly.*) Look! I got a proposition to make to you. I'm thinking of taking over the running of this place, you see? I think it could be run a bit more efficiently. I got a lot of ideas, a lot of plans. (*He eyes* DAVIES.) How would you like to stay on here, as caretaker?

DAVIES. What?

MICK. I'll be quite open with you. I could rely on a man like you around the place, keeping an eye on things.

DAVIES. Well now . . . wait a minute . . . I . . . I ain't never done no caretaking before, you know. . . .

MICK. Doesn't matter about that. It's just that you look a capable sort of man to me.

DAVIES. I am a capable sort of man. I mean to say, I've had plenty offers in my time, you know, there's no getting away from that.

MICK. Well, I could see before, when you took out that knife, that you wouldn't let anyone mess you about.

DAVIES. No one messes me about, man.

MICK. I mean, you've been in the services, haven't you?

DAVIES. The what?

MICK. You been in the services. You can tell by your stance.

DAVIES. Oh . . . yes. Spent half my life there, man. Overseas . . . like . . . serving . . . I was.

MICK. In the colonies, weren't you?

DAVIES. I was over there. I was one of the first over there.

MICK. That's it. You're just the man I been looking for.

DAVIES. What for?

MICK. Caretaker.

DAVIES. Yes, well . . . look . . . listen . . . who's the landlord here, him or you?

MICK. Me. I am. I got deeds to prove it.

DAVIES. Ah . . . (*Decisively.*) Well listen, I don't mind doing a bit of caretaking, I wouldn't mind looking after the place for you.

MICK. Of course, we'd come to a small financial agreement, mutually beneficial.

DAVIES. I leave you to reckon that out, like.

MICK. Thanks. There's only one thing.

DAVIES. What's that?

MICK. Can you give me any references?

DAVIES. Eh?

MICK. Just to satisfy my solicitor.

DAVIES. I got plenty of references. All I got to do is to go down to Sidcup tomorrow. I got all the references I want down there.

MICK. Where's that?

DAVIES. Sidcup. He ain't only got my references down there, he got all my papers down there. I know that place like the back of my hand. I'm going down there anyway, see what I mean, I got to get down there, or I'm done.

MICK. So we can always get hold of these references if we want them.

DAVIES. I'll be down there any day, I tell you. I was going down today, but I'm . . . I'm waiting for the weather to break.

MICK. Ah.

DAVIES. Listen. You can't pick me up a pair of good shoes, can you? I got a bad need for a good pair of shoes. I can't get anywhere without a pair of good shoes, see? Do you think there's any chance of you being able to pick me up a pair?

THE LIGHTS FADE TO BLACKOUT.
LIGHTS UP. *Morning.*
ASTON *is pulling on his trousers over long underwear. A slight grimace. He looks around at the head of his bed, takes a towel from the rail and waves it about. He pulls it down, goes to* DAVIES *and wakes him.* DAVIES *sits up abruptly.*

ASTON. You said you wanted me to get you up.

DAVIES. What for?

ASTON. You said you were thinking of going to Sidcup.

DAVIES. Ay, that'd be a good thing, if I got there.

ASTON. Doesn't look much of a day.

DAVIES. Ay, well, that's shot it, en't it?

ASTON. I . . . I didn't have a very good night again.

DAVIES. I slept terrible.

> *Pause.*

ASTON. You were making. . . .

DAVIES. Terrible. Had a bit of rain in the night, didn't it?

ASTON. Just a bit.

> *He goes to his bed, picks up a small plank and begins to sand-paper it.*

DAVIES. Thought so. Come in on my head.
> *Pause.*
Draught's blowing right in on my head, anyway.
> *Pause.*
Can't you close that window behind that sack?

ASTON. You could.

DAVIES. Well then, what about it, then? The rain's coming right in on my head.

ASTON. Got to have a bit of air.

> DAVIES *gets out of bed. He is wearing his trousers, waistcoat and vest.*

DAVIES (*putting on his sandals*). Listen. I've lived all my life in the air, boy. You don't have to tell me about air. What I'm saying is, there's too much air coming in that window when I'm asleep.

ASTON. Gets very stuffy in here without that window open.

ASTON *crosses to the chair, puts the plank on it, and continues sandpapering.*

DAVIES. Yes, but listen, you don't know what I'm telling you. That bloody rain, man, come right in on my head. Spoils my sleep. I could catch my death of cold with it, with that draught. That's all I'm saying. Just shut that window and no one's going to catch any colds, that's all I'm saying.

Pause.

ASTON. I couldn't sleep in here without that window open.

DAVIES. Yes, but what about me? What . . . what you got to say about my position?

ASTON. Why don't you sleep the other way round?

DAVIES. What do you mean?

ASTON. Sleep with your feet to the window.

DAVIES. What good would that do?

ASTON. The rain wouldn't come in on your head.

DAVIES. No, I couldn't do that. I couldn't do that.

Pause.

I mean, I got used to sleeping this way. It isn't me has to change, it's that window. You see, it's raining now. Look at it. It's coming down now.

Pause.

ASTON. I think I'll have a walk down to Goldhawk Road. I got talking to a man there. He had a saw bench. It looked in pretty good condition to me. Don't think it's much good to him.

Pause.

Have a walk down there, I think.

DAVIES. Listen to that. That's done my trip to Sidcup. Eh, what about closing that window now? It'll be coming in here.

ASTON. Close it for the time being.

DAVIES *closes the window and looks out.*

DAVIES. What's all that under that tarpaulin out there?

ASTON. Wood.

DAVIES. What for?

ASTON. To build my shed.

DAVIES *sits on his bed.*

DAVIES. You haven't come across that pair of shoes you was going to look out for me, have you?

ASTON. Oh. No. I'll see if I can pick some up today.

DAVIES. I can't go out in this with these, can I? I can't even go out and get a cup of tea.

ASTON. There's a café just along the road.

DAVIES. There may be, mate.

During ASTON'S *speech the room grows darker.*
By the close of the speech only ASTON *can be seen clearly.*
DAVIES *and all the other objects are in the shadow. The fade-down of the light must be as gradual, as protracted and as unobtrusive as possible.*

ASTON. I used to go there quite a bit. Oh, years ago now. But I stopped. I used to like that place. Spent quite a bit of time in there. That was before I went away. Just before. I think that . . . place had a lot to do with it. They were all . . . a good bit older than me. But they always used to listen. I thought . . . they understood what I said. I mean I used to talk to them. I talked too much. That was my mistake. The same in the factory. Standing there, or in the breaks, I used to . . . talk about things. And these men, they used to listen, whenever I . . . had anything to say. It was all right. The trouble was, I used to have kind of hallucinations.

They weren't hallucinations, they . . . I used to get the
feeling I could see things . . . very clearly . . . everything . . .
was so clear . . . everything used . . . everything used to
get very quiet . . . everything got very quiet . . . all this
. . . quiet . . . and . . . this clear sight . . . it was
. . . but maybe I was wrong. Anyway, someone must have
said something. I didn't know anything about it. And . . .
some kind of lie must have got around. And this lie went
round. I thought people started being funny. In that café.
The factory. I couldn't understand it. Then one day they
took me to a hospital, right outside London. They . . . got
me there. I didn't want to go. Anyway . . . I tried to get
out, quite a few times. But . . . it wasn't very easy. They
asked me questions, in there. Got me in and asked me all
sorts of questions. Well, I told them . . . when they
wanted to know . . . what my thoughts were. Hmmnn.
Then one day . . . this man . . . doctor, I suppose . . .
the head one . . . he was quite a man of . . . distinction
. . . although I wasn't so sure about that. He called me in.
He said . . . he told me I had something. He said they'd
concluded their examination. That's what he said. And he
showed me a pile of papers and he said that I'd got something, some complaint. He said . . . he just said that, you
see. You've got . . . this thing. That's your complaint.
And we've decided, he said, that in your interests there's
only one course we can take. He said . . . but I can't
. . . exactly remember . . . how he put it . . . he said,
we're going to do something to your brain. He said . . . if
we don't, you'll be in here for the rest of your life, but if we
do, you stand a chance. You can go out, he said, and live like
the others. What do you want to do to my brain, I said to
him. But he just repeated what he'd said. Well, I wasn't a
fool. I knew I was a minor. I knew he couldn't do anything
to me without getting permission. I knew he had to get
permission from my mother. So I wrote to her and told her

what they were trying to do. But she signed their form, you
see, giving them permission. I know that because he showed
me her signature when I brought it up. Well, that night I
tried to escape, that night. I spent five hours sawing at one
of the bars on the window in this ward. Right throughout
the dark. They used to shine a torch over the beds every
half hour. So I timed it just right. And then it was nearly
done, and a man had a . . . he had a fit, right next to me.
And they caught me, anyway. About a week later they
started to come round and do this thing to the brain. We
were all supposed to have it done, in this ward. And they
came round and did it one at a time. One a night. I was one
of the last. And I could see quite clearly what they did to the
others. They used to come round with these . . . I don't
know what they were . . . they looked like big pincers, with
wires on, the wires were attached to a little machine. It was
electric. They used to hold the man down, and this chief
. . . the chief doctor, used to fit the pincers, something like
earphones, he used to fit them on either side of the man's
skull. There was a man holding the machine, you see, and
he'd . . . turn it on, and the chief would just press these
pincers on either side of the skull and keep them there.
Then he'd take them off. They'd cover the man up . . .
and they wouldn't touch him again until later on. Some used
to put up a fight, but most of them didn't. They just lay
there. Well, they were coming round to me, and the night
they came I got up and stood against the wall. They told me
to get on the bed, and I knew they had to get me on the bed
because if they did it while I was standing up they might
break my spine. So I stood up and then one or two of them
came for me, well, I was younger then, I was much stronger
than I am now, I was quite strong then, I laid one of them
out and I had another one round the throat, and then
suddenly this chief had these pincers on my skull and I knew
he wasn't supposed to do it while I was standing up, that's

why I ..... anyway, he did it. So I did get out. I got out of the place ... but I couldn't walk very well. I don't think my spine was damaged. That was perfectly all right. The trouble was ... my thoughts ... had become very slow ... I couldn't think at all ... I couldn't ... get ... my thoughts ... together ... uuuhh ... I could ... never quite get it ... together. The trouble was, I couldn't hear what people were saying. I couldn't look to the right or the left, I had to look straight in front of me, because if I turned my head round ... I couldn't keep ... upright. And I had these headaches. I used to sit in my room. That was when I lived with my mother. And my brother. He was younger than me. And I laid everything out, in order, in my room, all the things I knew were mine, but I didn't die. The thing is, I should have been dead. I should have died. Anyway, I feel much better now. But I don't talk to people now. I steer clear of places like that café. I never go into them now. I don't talk to anyone ... like that. I've often thought of going back and trying to find the man who did that to me. But I want to do something first. I want to build that shed out in the garden.

Curtain

Act Three

Two weeks later.

> MICK *is lying on the floor, down left, his head resting on the rolled carpet, looking up at the ceiling.*
> DAVIES *is sitting in the chair, holding his pipe. He is wearing the smoking jacket. It is afternoon.*
> *Silence.*

DAVIES. I got a feeling he's done something to them cracks.

> *Pause.*

See, there's been plenty of rain in the last week, but it ain't been dripping into the bucket.

> *Pause.*

He must have tarred it over up there.

> *Pause.*

There was someone walking about on the roof the other night. It must have been him.

> *Pause.*

But I got a feeling he's tarred it over on the roof up there. Ain't said a word to me about it. Don't say a word to me.

> *Pause.*

He don't answer me when I talk to him.

> *He lights a match, holds it to his pipe, and blows it.*

He don't give me no knife!

> *Pause.*

He don't give me no knife to cut my bread.

> *Pause.*

How can I cut a loaf of bread without no knife?

> *Pause.*

It's an impossibility.

Pause.

MICK. You've got a knife.

DAVIES. What?

MICK. You've got a knife.

DAVIES. I got a knife, sure I got a knife, but how do you expect me to cut a good loaf of bread with that? That's not a bread-knife. It's nothing to do with cutting bread. I picked it up somewhere. I don't know where it's been, do I? No, what I want—

MICK. I know what you want.

Pause. DAVIES *rises and goes to the gas stove.*

DAVIES. What about this gas stove? He tells me it's not connected. How do I know it's not connected? Here I am, I'm sleeping right with it, I wake up in the middle of the night, I'm looking right into the oven, man! It's right next to my face, how do I know, I could be lying there in bed, it might blow up, it might do me harm!

Pause.

But he don't seem to take any notice of what I say to him. I told him the other day, see, I told him about them Blacks, about them Blacks coming up from next door, and using the lavatory. I told him, it was all dirty in there, all the banisters were dirty, they were black, all the lavatory was black. But what did he do? He's supposed to be in charge of it here, he had nothing to say, he hadn't got a word to say.

Pause.

Couple of weeks ago . . . he sat there, he give me a long chat . . . about a couple of weeks ago. A long chat he give me. Since then he ain't said hardly a word. He went on talking there . . . I don't know what he was . . . he wasn't looking at me, he wasn't talking to me, he don't care about me. He was talking to himself! That's all he worries about. I mean, you come up to me, you ask my advice, he wouldn't never do a thing like that. I mean, we don't have any conversation, you see? You can't live in the same room with someone who . . . who don't have any conversation with you.

Pause.

I just can't get the hang of him.

Pause.

You and me, we could get this place going.

MICK (*ruminatively*). Yes, you're quite right. Look what I could do with this place.

Pause.

I could turn this place into a penthouse. For instance . . . this room. This room you could have as the kitchen. Right size, nice window, sun comes in. I'd have . . . I'd have teal-blue, copper and parchment linoleum squares. I'd have those colours re-echoed in the walls. I'd offset the kitchen units with charcoal-grey worktops. Plenty of room for cupboards for the crockery. We'd have a small wall cupboard, a large wall cupboard, a corner wall cupboard with revolving shelves. You wouldn't be short of cupboards. You could put the dining-room across the landing, see? Yes. Venetian blinds on the window, cork floor, cork tiles. You could have an off-white pile linen rug, a table in . . . in afromosia teak veneer, sideboard with matt black drawers, curved chairs with cushioned seats, armchairs in oatmeal tweed, a beech frame settee with a woven sea-grass seat, white-topped heat-resistant coffee table, white tile surround. Yes. Then the bedroom. What's a bedroom? It's a retreat. It's a place to go for rest and peace. So you want quiet decoration. The lighting functional. Furniture . . . mahogany and rosewood. Deep azure-blue carpet, unglazed blue and white curtains, a bedspread with a pattern of small blue roses on a white ground, dressing-table with a lift-up top containing a plastic tray, table lamp of white raffia . . . (MICK *sits up*.) it wouldn't be a flat it'd be a palace.

DAVIES. I'd say it would, man.

MICK. A palace.

DAVIES. Who would live there?

MICK. I would. My brother and me.

>   *Pause.*

DAVIES. What about me?

MICK (*quietly*). All this junk here, it's no good to anyone. It's just a lot of old iron, that's all. Clobber. You couldn't make a home out of this. There's no way you could arrange it. It's junk. He could never sell it, either, he wouldn't get tuppence for it.

>   *Pause.*

Junk.

>   *Pause.*

But he doesn't seem to be interested in what I got in mind, that's the trouble. Why don't you have a chat with him, see if he's interested?

DAVIES. Me?

MICK. Yes. You're a friend of his.

DAVIES. He's no friend of mine.

MICK. You're living in the same room with him, en't you?

DAVIES. He's no friend of mine. You don't know where you are with him. I mean, with a bloke like you, you know where you are.

>   MICK *looks at him.*

I mean, you got your own ways, I'm not saying you ain't got your own ways, anyone can see that. You may have some funny ways, but that's the same with all of us, but with him it's different, see? I mean at least with you, the thing with you is you're . . .

MICK. Straightforward.

DAVIES. That's it, you're straightforward.

MICK. Yes.

DAVIES. But with him, you don't know what he's up to half the time!

MICK. Uh.

DAVIES. He's got no feelings!

Pause.

See, what I need is a clock! I need a clock to tell the time! How can I tell the time without a clock? I can't do it! I said to him, I said, look here, what about getting in a clock, so's I can tell what time it is? I mean, if you can't tell what time you're at you don't know where you are, you understand my meaning? See, what I got to do now, if I'm walking about outside, I got to get my eye on a clock, and keep the time in my head for when I come in. But that's no good, I mean I'm not in here five minutes and I forgotten it. I forgotten what time it was!

DAVIES *walks up and down the room.*

Look at it this way. If I don't feel well I have a bit of a lay down, then, when I wake up, I don't know what time it is to go and have a cup of tea! You see, it's not so bad when I'm coming in. I can see the clock on the corner, the moment I'm stepping into the house I know what the time is, but when I'm *in*! It's when I'm *in* . . . that I haven't the foggiest idea what time it is!

Pause.

No, what I need is a clock in here, in this room, and then I stand a bit of a chance. But he don't give me one.

DAVIES *sits in the chair.*

He wakes me up! He wakes me up in the middle of the night! Tells me I'm making noises! I tell you I've half a mind to give him a mouthful one of these days.

MICK. He don't let you sleep?

DAVIES. He don't let me sleep! He wakes me up!

MICK. That's terrible.

DAVIES. I been plenty of other places. They always let

me sleep. It's the same the whole world over. Except here.

MICK. Sleep's essential. I've always said that.

DAVIES. You're right, it's essential. I get up in the morning, I'm worn out! I got business to see to. I got to move myself, I got to sort myself out, I got to get fixed up. But when I wake up in the morning, I ain't got no energy in me. And on top of that I ain't got no clock.

MICK. Yes.

DAVIES (*standing, moving*). He goes out, I don't know where he goes to, where's he go, he never tells me. We used to have a bit of a chat, not any more. I never see him, he goes out, he comes in late, next thing I know he's shoving me about in the middle of the night.

Pause.

Listen! I wake up in the morning . . . I wake up in the morning and he's smiling at me! He's standing there, looking at me, smiling! I can see him, you see, I can see him through the blanket. He puts on his coat, he turns himself round, he looks down at my bed, there's a smile on his face! What the hell's he smiling at? What he don't know is that I'm watching him through that blanket. He don't know that! He don't know I can see him, he thinks I'm asleep, but I got my eye on him all the time through the blanket, see? But he don't know that! He just looks at me and he smiles, but he don't know that I can see him doing it!

Pause.

(*Bending, close to* MICK.) No, what you want to do, you want to speak to him, see? I got . . . I got that worked out. You want to tell him . . . that we got ideas for this place, we could build it up, we could get it started. You see, I could decorate it out for you, I could give you a hand in doing it . . . between us.

Pause.

Where do you live now, then?

MICK. Me? Oh, I've got a little place. Not bad. Everything

laid on. You must come up and have a drink some time.
Listen to some Tchaikovsky.

DAVIES. No, you see, you're the bloke who wants to talk to
him. I mean, you're his brother.

Pause.

MICK. Yes . . . maybe I will.

A door bangs.
MICK *rises, goes to the door and exits.*

DAVIES. Where you going? This is him!

Silence.
DAVIES *stands, then goes to the window and looks out.*
ASTON *enters. He is carrying a paper bag. He takes off his
overcoat, opens the bag and takes out a pair of shoes.*

ASTON. Pair of shoes.
DAVIES (*turning*). What?
ASTON. I picked them up. Try them.
DAVIES. Shoes? What sort?
ASTON. They might do you.

DAVIES *comes down stage, takes off his sandals and tries the
shoes on. He walks about, waggling his feet, bends, and
presses the leather.*

DAVIES. No, they're not right.
ASTON. Aren't they?
DAVIES. No, they don't fit.
ASTON. Mmnn.

Pause.

DAVIES. Well, I'll tell you what, they might do . . . until I
get another pair.

Pause.

Where's the laces?
ASTON. No laces.
DAVIES. I can't wear them without laces.

ASTON. I just got the shoes.

DAVIES. Well now, look that puts the lid on it, don't it? I mean, you couldn't keep these shoes on right without a pair of laces. The only way to keep a pair of shoes on, if you haven't got no laces, is to tighten the foot, see? Walk about with a tight foot, see? Well, that's no good for the foot. Puts a bad strain on the foot. If you can do the shoes up proper there's less chance of you getting a strain.

ASTON *goes round to the top of his bed.*

ASTON. I might have some somewhere.

DAVIES. You see what I'm getting at?

Pause.

ASTON. Here's some. (*He hands them to* DAVIES.)

DAVIES. These are brown.

ASTON. That's all I got.

DAVIES. These shoes are black.

ASTON *does not answer.*

Well, they can do, anyway, until I get another pair.

DAVIES *sits in the chair and begins to lace his shoes.*

Maybe they'll get me down to Sidcup tomorrow. If I get down there I'll be able to sort myself out.

Pause.

I've been offered a good job. Man has offered it to me, he's . . . he's got plenty of ideas. He's got a bit of a future. But they want my papers, you see, they want my references. I'd have to get down to Sidcup before I could get hold of them. That's where they are, see. Trouble is, getting there. That's my problem. The weather's dead against it.

ASTON *quietly exits, unnoticed.*

Don't know as these shoes'll be much good. It's a hard road, I been down there before. Coming the other way, like. Last time I left there, it was . . . last time . . . getting on a while back . . . the road was bad, the rain was coming down, lucky I didn't die there on the road, but I got here, I kept going, all along . . . yes . . . I kept going all along. But all the same, I can't go on like this, what I got to do, I got to get back there, find this man—

He turns and looks about the room.

Christ! That bastard, he ain't even listening to me!

BLACKOUT.
DIM LIGHT THROUGH THE WINDOW.
It is night. ASTON *and* DAVIES *are in bed,* DAVIES *groaning.* ASTON *sits up, gets out of bed, switches on the light, goes over to* DAVIES *and shakes him.*

ASTON. Hey, stop it, will you? I can't sleep.

DAVIES. What? What? What's going on?

ASTON. You're making noises.

DAVIES. I'm an old man, what do you expect me to do, stop breathing?

ASTON. You're making noises.

DAVIES. What do you expect me to do, stop breathing?

ASTON *goes to his bed, and puts on his trousers.*

ASTON. I'll get a bit of air.

DAVIES. What do you expect me to do? I tell you, mate, I'm not surprised they took you in. Waking an old man up in the middle of the night, you must be off your nut! Giving me bad dreams, who's responsible, then, for me having bad dreams? If you wouldn't keep mucking me about I wouldn't make no noises! How do you expect me to sleep peaceful when you keep poking me all the time? What do you want me to do, stop breathing?

He throws the cover off and gets out of bed, wearing his vest, waistcoat and trousers.

It's getting so freezing in here I have to keep my trousers on to go to bed. I never done that before in my life. But that's

what I got to do here. Just because you won't put in any
bleeding heating! I've had just about enough with you
mucking me about. I've seen better days than you have, man.
Nobody ever got me inside one of them places, anyway. I'm
a sane man! So don't you start mucking me about. I'll be all
right as long as you keep your place. Just you keep your
place, that's all. Because I can tell you, your brother's got his
eye on you. He knows all about you. I got a friend there,
don't you worry about that. I got a true pal there. Treating
me like dirt! Why'd you invite me in here in the first place if
you was going to treat me like this? You think you're better
than me you got another think coming. I know enough.
They had you inside one of them places before, they can have
you inside again. Your brother's got his eye on you! They
can put the pincers on your head again, man! They can
have them on again! Any time. All they got to do is get the
word. They'd carry you in there, boy. They'd come here and
pick you up and carry you in! They'd keep you fixed! They'd
put them pincers on your head, they'd have you fixed!
They'd take one look at all this junk I got to sleep with they'd
know you were a creamer. That was the greatest mistake they
made, you take my tip, letting you get out of that place.
Nobody knows what you're at, you go out you come in,
nobody knows what you're at! Well, nobody messes me
about for long. You think I'm going to do your dirty work?
Haaaaahhhhh! You better think again! You want me to do
all the dirty work all up and down them stairs just so I can
sleep in this lousy filthy hole every night? Not me, boy. Not
for you boy. You don't know what you're doing half the
time. You're up the creek! You're half off! You can tell it by
looking at you. Who ever saw you slip me a few bob?
Treating me like a bloody animal! I never been inside a
nuthouse!

ASTON *makes a slight move towards him.* DAVIES *takes his
knife from his back pocket.*

Don't come nothing with me, mate. I got this here. I used
it. I used it. Don't come it with me.

A pause. They stare at each other.

Mind what you do now.

Pause.

Don't you try anything with me.

Pause.

ASTON. I . . . I think it's about time you found somewhere
else. I don't think we're hitting it off.

DAVIES. Find somewhere else?

ASTON. Yes.

DAVIES. Me? You talking to me? Not me, man! You!

ASTON. What?

DAVIES. You! You better find somewhere else!

ASTON. I live here. You don't.

DAVIES. Don't I? Well, I live here. I been offered a job here.

ASTON. Yes . . . well, I don't think you're really suitable.

DAVIES. Not suitable? Well, I can tell you, there's someone
here thinks I am suitable. And I'll tell you. I'm staying on
here as caretaker! Get it! Your brother, he's told me, see,
he's told me the job is mine. Mine! So that's where I am.
I'm going to be his caretaker.

ASTON. My brother?

DAVIES. He's staying, he's going to run this place, and I'm
staying with him.

ASTON. Look. If I give you . . . a few bob you can get down
to Sidcup.

DAVIES. You build your shed first! A few bob! When I can
earn a steady wage here! You build your stinking shed first!
That's what!

 ASTON *stares at him.*

ASTON. That's not a stinking shed.

 Silence.

 ASTON *moves to him.*

It's clean. It's all good wood. I'll get it up. No trouble.

DAVIES. Don't come too near!

ASTON. You've no reason to call that shed stinking.

DAVIES *points the knife.*

You stink.

DAVIES. What!

ASTON. You've been stinking the place out.

DAVIES. Christ, you say that to me!

ASTON. For days. That's one reason I can't sleep.

DAVIES. You call me that! You call me stinking!

ASTON. You better go.

DAVIES. I'LL STINK YOU!

He thrusts his arm out, the arm trembling, the knife pointing at ASTON'S *stomach.* ASTON *does not move. Silence.* DAVIES' *arm moves no further. They stand.*

I'll stink you. . . .

Pause.

ASTON. Get your stuff.

DAVIES *draws the knife in to his chest, breathing heavily.* ASTON *goes to* DAVIES' *bed, collects his bag and puts a few of* DAVIES' *things into it.*

DAVIES. You ain't . . . you ain't got the right . . . Leave that alone, that's mine!

DAVIES *takes the bag and presses the contents down.*

All right . . . I been offered a job here . . . you wait . . . (*He puts on his smoking-jacket.*) . . you wait . . . your brother . . . he'll sort you out . . . you call me that . . . you call me that . . . no one's ever called me that ˙ . . (*He puts on his overcoat.*) You'll be sorry you called me that . . . . you ain't heard the last of this . . . (*He picks up his bag and goes to the door.*) You'll be sorry you called me that. . . .

He opens the door, ASTON *watching him.*

Now I know who I can trust.

DAVIES *goes out.* ASTON *stands.*
BLACKOUT.
LIGHTS UP. *Early evening.*
Voices on the stairs.
MICK *and* DAVIES *enter.*

DAVIES. Stink! You hear that! Me! I told you what he said, didn't I? Stink! You hear that? That's what he said to me!

MICK. Tch, tch, tch.

DAVIES. That's what he said to me.

MICK. You don't stink.

DAVIES. No, sir!

MICK. If you stank I'd be the first one to tell you.

DAVIES. I told him, I told him he . . . I said to him, you ain't heard the last of this man! I said, don't you forget your brother. I told him you'd be coming along to sort him out. He don't know what he's started, doing that. Doing that to me. I said to him, I said to him, he'll be along, your brother'll be along, he's got sense, not like you—

MICK. What do you mean?

DAVIES. Eh?

MICK. You saying my brother hasn't got any sense?

DAVIES. What? What I'm saying is, you got ideas for this place, all this . . . all this decorating, see? I mean, he's got no right to order me about. I take orders from you, I do my caretaking for you, I mean, you look upon me . . . you don't treat me like a lump of dirt . . . we can both . . . we can both see him for what he is.

Pause.

MICK. What did he say then, when you told him I'd offered you the job as caretaker?

DAVIES. He . . . he said . . . he said . . . something about. . . he lived here.

MICK. Yes, he's got a point, en he?

DAVIES. A point! This is your house, en't? You let him live here!

MICK. I could tell him to go, I suppose.

DAVIES. That's what I'm saying.

MICK. Yes. I could tell him to go. I mean, I'm the landlord. On the other hand, he's the sitting tenant. Giving him notice, you see, what it is, it's a technical matter, that's what it is. It depends how you regard this room. I mean it depends whether you regard this room as furnished or unfurnished. See what I mean?

DAVIES. No, I don't.

MICK. All this furniture, you see, in here, it's all his, except the beds, of course. So what it is, it's a fine legal point, that's what it is.

Pause.

DAVIES. I tell you he should go back where he come from!

MICK (*turning to look at him*). Come from?

DAVIES. Yes.

MICK. Where did he come from?

DAVIES. Well ... he ... he. ...

MICK. You get a bit out of your depth sometimes, don't you?
Pause.
(*Rising, briskly.*) Well, anyway, as things stand, I don't mind having a go at doing up the place. ...

DAVIES. That's what I wanted to hear!

MICK. No, I don't mind.
He turns to face DAVIES.
But you better be as good as you say you are.

DAVIES. What do you mean?

MICK. Well, you say you're an interior decorator, you'd better be a good one.

DAVIES. A what?

MICK. What do you mean, a what? A decorator. An interior decorator.

DAVIES. Me? What do you mean? I never touched that. I never been that.

MICK. You've never what?

DAVIES. No, no, not me, man. I'm not an interior decorator. I been too busy. Too many other things to do, you see. But I . . . but I could always turn my hand to most things . . . give me . . . give me a bit of time to pick it up.

MICK. I don't want you to pick it up. I want a first-class experienced interior decorator. I thought you were one.

DAVIES. Me? Now wait a minute— wait a minute—you got the wrong man.

MICK. How could I have the wrong man? You're the only man I've spoken to. You're the only man I've told, about my dreams, about my deepest wishes, you're the only one I've told, and I only told you because I understood you were an experienced first-class professional interior and exterior decorator.

DAVIES. Now look here—

MICK. You mean you wouldn't know how to fit teal-blue, copper and parchment linoleum squares and have those colours re-echoed in the walls?

DAVIES. Now, look here, where'd you get—?

MICK. You wouldn't be able to decorate out a table in afro-mosia teak veneer, an armchair in oatmeal tweed and a beech frame settee with a woven sea-grass seat?

DAVIES. I never said that!

MICK. Christ! I must have been under a false impression!

DAVIES. I never said it!

MICK. You're a bloody impostor, mate!

DAVIES. Now you don't want to say that sort of thing to me. You took me on here as caretaker. I was going to give you a helping hand, that's all, for a small . . for a small wage, I never said nothing about that . . . you start calling me names—

MICK. What is your name?

DAVIES. Don't start that—

MICK. No, what's your real name?

DAVIES. My real name's Davies.

MICK. What's the name you go under?

DAVIES. Jenkins!

MICK. You got two names. What about the rest? Eh? Now come on, why did you tell me all this dirt about you being an interior decorator?

DAVIES. I didn't tell you nothing! Won't you listen to what I'm saying?

Pause.

It was him who told you. It was your brother who must have told you. He's nutty! He'd tell you anything, out of spite, he's nutty, he's half way gone, it was him who told you.

MICK *walks slowly to him.*

MICK. What did you call my brother?

DAVIES. When?

MICK. He's what?

DAVIES. I . . . now get this straight. . . .

MICK. Nutty? Who's nutty?

Pause.

Did you call my brother nutty? My brother. That's a bit of
. . . . that's a bit of an impertinent thing to say, isn't it?

DAVIES. But he says so himself!

MICK *walks slowly round* DAVIES' *figure, regarding him, once. He circles him, once.*

MICK. What a strange man you are. Aren't you? You're really strange. Ever since you come into this house there's been nothing but trouble. Honest. I can take nothing you say at face value. Every word you speak is open to any number of different interpretations. Most of what you say is lies. You're violent, you're erratic, you're just completely unpredictable. You're nothing else but a wild animal, when you come down to it. You're a barbarian. And to put the old tin lid on it, you stink from arse-hole to breakfast time. Look at it. You come here recommending yourself as an interior decorator, whereupon I take you on, and what happens? You make a long speech about all the references you've got down at Sidcup, and what happens? I haven't noticed you go down to Sidcup to obtain them. It's all most regrettable but it looks as though I'm compelled to pay you off for your caretaking work. Here's half a dollar.

He feels in his pocket, takes out a half-crown and tosses it at DAVIES' *feet.* DAVIES *stands still.* MICK *walks to the gas stove and picks up the Buddha.*

DAVIES (*slowly*). All right then . . . you do that . . . you do it . . . if that's what you want. . . .

MICK. THAT'S WHAT I WANT!

He hurls the Buddha against the gas stove. It breaks.

(*Passionately.*) Anyone would think this house was all I got to worry about. I got plenty of other things I can worry about. I've got other things. I've got plenty of other interests. I've got my own business to build up, haven't I? I got to think about expanding . . . in all directions. I don't stand still. I'm moving about, all the time. I'm moving . . . all the time. I've got to think about the future. I'm not worried about this house. I'm not interested. My brother can worry about it. He can do it up, he can decorate it, he can do what he likes with it. I'm not bothered. I thought I was doing him a favour, letting him live here. He's got his own ideas. Let him have them. I'm going to chuck it in.

Pause.

DAVIES. What about me?

Silence. MICK *does not look at him.*
A door bangs.

Silence. They do not move.

ASTON *comes in. He closes the door, moves into the room and faces* MICK. *They look at each other. Both are smiling, faintly.*

MICK (*beginning to speak to* ASTON). Look. . . uh . . .
He stops, goes to the door and exits. ASTON *leaves the door open, crosses behind* DAVIES, *sees the broken Buddha, and looks at the pieces for a moment. He then goes to his bed, takes off his overcoat, sits, takes the screwdriver and plug and pokes the plug.*

DAVIES. I just come back for my pipe.

ASTON. Oh yes.

DAVIES. I got out and . . . half way down I . . . I suddenly . . . found out . . . you see . . . that I hadn't got my pipe. So I come back to get it. . . .

Pause. He moves to ASTON.

That ain't the same plug, is it, you been . . .?

Pause.

Still can't get anywhere with it, eh?

Pause.

Well, if you . . . persevere, in my opinion, you'll probably . . .

Pause.

Listen. . . .

Pause.

You didn't mean that, did you, about me stinking, did you?

Pause.

Did you? You been a good friend to me. You took me in. You took me in, you didn't ask me no questions, you give me a bed, you been a mate to me. Listen. I been thinking, why I made all them noises, it was because of the draught, see, that draught was on me as I was sleeping, made me make noises without me knowing it, so I been thinking, what I mean to say, if you was to give me your bed, and you have my bed, there's not all that difference between them, they're the same sort of bed, if I was to have yourn, you sleep, wherever bed you're in, so you have mine, I have yourn, and that'll be all right, I'll be out of the draught, see, I mean, you don't mind a bit of wind, you need a bit of air, I can understand that, you being in that place that time, with all them doctors and all they done, closed up, I know them places, too hot, you see, they're always too hot, I had a peep in one once, nearly suffocated me, so I reckon that'd be the best way out of it, we swap beds, and then we could get down to what we was saying, I'd look after the place for you, I'd keep an eye on it for you, for you, like, not for the other . . . not for . . . for your brother, you see, not for him, for you, I'll be your man, you say the word, just say the word. . . .

  Pause.

What do you think of this I'm saying?

  Pause.

ASTON. No, I like sleeping in this bed.

DAVIES. But you don't understand my meaning!

ASTON. Anyway, that one's my brother's bed.

DAVIES. Your brother?

ASTON. Any time he stays here. This is my bed. It's the only bed I can sleep in.

DAVIES. But your brother's gone! He's gone!

  Pause.

ASTON. No. I couldn't change beds.

DAVIES. But you don't understand my meaning!

ASTON. Anyway, I'm going to be busy. I've got that shed to get up. If I don't get it up now it'll never go up. Until it's up I can't get started.

DAVIES. I'll give you a hand to put up your shed, that's what I'll do!

  Pause.

I'll give you a hand! We'll both put up that shed together!
See? Get it done in next to no time! Do you see what
I'm saying?

Pause.

ASTON. No. I can get it up myself.

DAVIES. But listen. I'm with you, I'll be here, I'll do it for
you!

Pause.

We'll do it together!

Pause.

Christ, we'll change beds!

ASTON *moves to the window and stands with his back to*
DAVIES.

You mean you're throwing me out? You can't do that.
Listen man, listen man, I don't mind, you see, I don't mind,
I'll stay, I don't mind, I'll tell you what, if you don't want
to change beds, we'll keep it as it is, I'll stay in the same bed,
maybe if I can get a stronger piece of sacking, like, to go
over the window, keep out the draught, that'll do it, what do
you say, we'll keep it as it is?

Pause.

ASTON. No.

DAVIES. Why . . . not?

ASTON *turns to look at him.*

ASTON. You make too much noise.

DAVIES. But . . . but . . . look . . . listen . . . listen here . . .
I mean. . . .

ASTON *turns back to the window.*

What am I going to do?

Pause.

What shall I do?

Pause.

Where am I going to go?

Pause.

If you want me to go . . . I'll go. You just say the word.

Pause.

I'll tell you what though . . . them shoes . . . them shoes you give me . . . they're working out all right . . . they're all right. Maybe I could . . . get down. . . .

ASTON *remains still, his back to him, at the window.*

Listen . . . if I . . . got down . . . if I was to . . . get my papers . . . would you . . . would you let . . . would you . . . if I got down . . . and got my. . . .

Long silence.

Curtain.

Notes

(These notes are intended to serve the needs of overseas students as well as those of English-born readers.)

6 *a mound* — a heap of objects piled on top of each other.
6 *shopping trolley* — a small cart on wheels used for carrying goods around or back from the shops.
6 *a statue of Buddha* — a statue of the god-figure associated with enlightenment and peace in a religious movement founded in India. The statue is later smashed by Mick.
6 *a clothes horse* — a frame over which clothes can be hung, often to help them dry out.
6 *electrolux* — the name of a common make of vacuum-cleaner for carpets.

Act I

7 *a pinstripe suit* — a man's suit made from dark material patterned with thin, light-coloured stripes running vertically and — when in good condition — considered appropriate wear for businessmen.
7 *a good sit down* — a welcome rest.
8 *tea-break* — a short period, generally set aside in the middle of the morning and the afternoon, to allow workers time for a cup of tea or coffee.
8 *all them aliens* — all those foreigners. In many dialects 'those' is replaced by 'them'. The choice of 'aliens' emphasises Davies's sense of their being different from himself, intruders.
8 *doing me out of* — depriving by underhand or deceitful means, cheating.
8 *treating me like dirt* — behaving as if I were of no importance, insultingly.
8 *come at me* — threatened to attack me. In many dialects, or slang, 'came' is replaced by 'come'.
8 *loosen myself up* — get into good physical condition, work off any stiffness of the muscles as an athletic must in training.

8   *got done in* — have been killed (slang).

8   *knocked off* — stolen (slang).

8   *Great West Road* — one of the main roads leading out of London to the west.

8   *I told him* — I told him plainly and forcefully what I thought of him.

9   *have a go at* — try to attack.

9   *filthy skate* — disgusting and contemptible person (slang).

9   *I've had dinner with the best* — the suggestion that Davies has been invited as a guest into the homes of wealthy and respected people is ironic and incongruous in view of his apparent poverty and irregular way of life.

9   *toe-rags* — people of no account, beggars (slang).

9   *mate* — Cockney term of address, meaning simply 'friend' or 'man'.

9   *been on the road* — travelling as a tramp.

9   *I keep myself up* — I take care of myself, keep clean and in good condition.

9   *handy* — competent, able to do a variety of manual tasks.

9   *take any liberties* — treat with disrespect, take advantage of.

9   *had a few attacks* — suffered bouts of ill health. There is also the suggestion of violence in the phrase, consistent with the tramp's general attitude.

9   *I only got the end of it* — I only heard or witnessed the last moments.

9   *parks* — hands over with little ceremony (slang).

9   *take it out the back* — take it to the dustbins outside the back entrance.

9   *wasn't engaged* — was not hired for that job.

9   *git* — bastard, worthless individual. Colloquial term of abuse.

10   *got the same standing* — have the same status, are of equal rank or importance.

10   *a Scotch* — a Scotsman. Davies's resentment seems to include anyone not English.

10   *got an eye* — had a look at.

10   *guvnor* — a colloquial corruption of 'governor', meaning 'employer' or 'proprietor'.

10   *give me the bullet* — dismissed me from my job (slang). Again Davies uses an idiom suggestive of violence. 'Give' should be 'gave' in educated speech.

10   *got my rights* — Davies is aware that any worker has certain rights established by legislation to protect him from exploitation or unfair dismissal by his employer.

10 *a bit of fair play* — fair and just treatment according to the rules of society, the law, or common humanity.

10 *if he'd have landed* — if he had succeeded in hitting me (slang).

10 *I'll get him* — I'll get my revenge on him, punish him violently.

10 *lousy* — disgusting, loathsome, originally meaning 'infested with lice' (slang).

10 *blasted . . . bleeding* — colloquial expressions of strong annoyance or dislike, equivalent to 'damned' and 'bloody'.

10 *having a poke around* — searching inside, prying into, investigating (slang).

10 *I'll pop down* — make a short visit (colloquial).

11 *like* — in several dialects 'like' is used as an interjection meaning, rather vaguely, 'if you see what I mean'.

11 *worth a few bob* — of some value. 'Bob' was a common colloquialism for the now out-dated English coin, the shilling — approximately equal in value to the modern five-pence piece.

11 *kipping out* — sleeping out-of-doors (slang).

12 *need a lot of doing to* — require considerable redecoration.

12 *out of commission* — not being used.

12 *Get away* — You must be joking! Don't talk nonsense! (cockney slang).

12 *that caff* — that café, snack bar. The corruption of the word emphasises the cheap or even squalid character of the place.

13 *Blacks* — colloquial expression describing people of African or Asian extraction and often used in the fifties and sixties to convey the speaker's racial prejudices.

13 *knick-knacks* — trinkets, small and generally merely ornamental objects.

13 *let me down* — disappointed me, did not do what was expected of them.

13 *In the convenience* — in the public toilets. Davies's friend was employed to clean and supervise the public lavatory.

13 *slipped me* — handed over to me when no-one was looking (slang).

13 *to be knocking about* — to be wandering about (slang).

13 *Luton* — a town just north of London, associated with industry rather than thought of as a likely location for a monastery.

13 *It's life and death* — a colloquial overstatement for emphasis, meaning that it is a matter of great importance, necessary to the tramps's way of life.

14 *Acton* — a district of west London.

14 *not bad trim* — in quite good condition.

14 *enough to keep me on my way* — good enough for me to walk a reasonable distance in.

14 *they're nearly out* — these are nearly worn through, in holes.

14 *Piss off* — an abusive and vulgar way of saying 'Go away' — not what a monk might be expected to say.

14 *without a bite* — without food.

15 *could have ate it* — corruption of 'could have eaten it'.

15 *get off out of it* — get away from here, stop bothering us (slang).

15 *your mother superior* — the principal of a convent. Since Davies is talking to a monk rather than a nun, he should say 'father superior', so he is either being deliberately offensive or simply displaying his ignorance.

15 *I cleared out* — I left the place quickly.

15 *Watford* and *Hendon*— suburbs to the north of London.

15 *the North Circular* — a main road circling the northern suburbs of London and acting as a route for vehicles wishing to by-pass the city.

15 *some bloke* — some man or other (slang).

15 *to flog me* — to sell me (slang).

15 *some suede* — some shoes made of suede leather and so not very hard-wearing.

16 *not much cop* — not of good quality, not much use (slang).

16 *what I can look out* — what I can find.

16 *get fixed up* — arrange his affairs, find shelter and employment.

16 *waiting for the weather to break* — waiting for a change in the weather, for conditions to improve.

16 *I picked it up* — I acquired it for little or no money. Accumulating miscellaneous objects is characteristic of Aston, some evidently useful, some bizarre. He has 'picked up' Davies in much the same way.

16 *come in handy* — prove to be useful.

17 *Buddha* — (see note to p. 6).

17 *en't they* — Cockney corruption of 'aren't they'.

18 *It's a ton weight* — it's very heavy. Although a ton is a specific measurement of weight, the term is generally used merely for emphasis.

18 *fair's fair* — a colloquial expression conveying a rather vague idea of what it is right and fitting to do under the prevailing circumstances.

19 *I'm a bit short* — I haven't enough money for my needs.

19 *Here's a few bob* — (see note on p. 11). Later Davies denies that Aston ever gave him any money (p. 67).

19 *A Guinness* — a strong, dark beer from Ireland.

19 *Sidcup* — a commuter town in Kent, to the south-east of London. It is an unexpected place for the tramp to name as his goal, the place which he will reach only with difficulty if at all in his search for documents to confirm his identity and establish him properly in society.

19 *I got my papers there* — the official documents which Davies claims to have left with someone in Sidcup. He is never more specific about them.

20 *I'm stuck* — I'm unable to do anything.

20 *an insurance card* — a National Insurance card on which a stamp should be stuck each week that a person is employed to indicate that the tax has been paid which will entitle that individual to welfare benefits from the state should he be in need.

20 *have me in the nick* — put me in prison (slang).

20 *the nigs* — shortened form of 'niggers', originally a contemptuous reference to negroes but here used as a term of abuse for his employers, who, he claims, have not fulfilled their legal obligation to provide stamps for his National Insurance card.

20 *to go into it* — to investigate the matter.

20 *waiting for the weather to break* — (see note to p. 16).

21 *in the war* — during the Second World War, 1939—45.

21 *a bit done in* — tired, worn out, exhausted (slang).

21 *straightens his bed* — smooths out the sheets and blankets to make the bed look neat.

22 *dead out* — sleeping heavily, unaware of anything.

22 *jabbering* — making rapid, indistinct sounds. The word is often applied to the noise made by monkeys, which may explain Davies's hostile reaction.

23 *where's the sense in it* — what reason is there for it.

23 *You got hold of the wrong bloke* — you're accusing the wrong man. Since Davies was the only other person in the room with Aston, this reply is absurd.

24 *a jig saw . . . fret saw* — both types of narrow saw used for cutting decorative patterns into wood.

24 *They're very handy* — they're very useful.

25 *Get out of it* — stick to facts, don't talk nonsense.

25 *To come out with it just like that* — to make an unexpected remark without introducing the topic gradually.

25 *I been around* — I've travelled about and have a wide
experience of life.

25 *darkly* — so as to give nothing away, reveal no information,
but also with suspicion and even hostility.

25 *lose a bit of track* — a distortion of the idiom 'to lose track of
something' which means 'to be unable to follow an argument or
idea', or 'to misplace something and be unable to find it again'.
Davies cannot remember his past clearly, or is unwilling to do so.

26 *I don't go in for them things much* — I haven't much use for
such things.

26 *It's not connected* — it's not supplied with gas; the pipe has
been shut off or detached from the main supply.

26 *take any liberties* — (see note to p. 9).

27 *Wembley* — suburb in the north-west of London.

27 *a caff* — (see note to p. 12).

27 *get fixed up* — get a job.

27 *short-handed* — with too few people to cope with the work to
be done.

27 *the right kind of people* — Davies evidently means people like
himself, not immigrants.

28 *grimaces* — pulls a face to suggest unease, dislike.

28 *rummages* — searches about in, disturbing the contents.

29 *writhes* — twists and wriggles as if in pain.

29 *clothes horse* — (see note to p. 6).

29 *What's the game?* — What scheme, probably illegal or at least
dishonest, are you trying out?

Act II

30 *I'm awfully glad* — 'awfully' is an alternative to 'very' or
'extremely', used here by Mick to imitate the manners of the upper
classes of society.

31 *Jen . . . kins* — by splitting the word up in this way, Mick not
only conveys that he is assessing its likely accuracy and matching it
against his memories to see whether anything is known about the
man who claims it as his name (as a policeman might check
through criminal records when interviewing a suspect), he also
destroys the word's coherence, rendering it either nonsensical or
sinister.

31 *my uncle's brother* — this must refer either to a second uncle,
or to Mick's father (see the section on 'Interpretations' in the
Introduction). Throughout this speech Mick's use of language is a

disconcerting blend of familiar phrases in odd contexts and sudden, apparently absurd non-sequiturs linked only by the persistent idea of his 'uncle's brother', Sid.

31 *an eye for the girls* — enjoyed looking at pretty girls.

31 *run-ups in the drawing-room* — Mick's use of 'drawing-room' rather than 'lounge' or 'sitting-room' is part of his affectation of upper class manners.

31 *penchant* — liking for. Another deliberately affected choice of word.

31 *fruit cake . . . nuts . . . stop-watch* — as well as their literal meaning, these words also contain sexual innuendoes.

31 *chucked him out* — expelled him. The expression could also mean that Sid was forcibly thrown out into the street from one of the hostels for the homeless run by the Salvation Army.

31 *Salvation Army* — a Christian organisation founded in 1865 to combat poverty, drunkenness and the decline of religious faith.

31 *Used to go in number four for Beckenham Reserves* — 'go in number four' is a cricketing term, meaning 'be the fourth man to bat'. Beckenham Reserves, on the other hand, is the name of a not particularly distinguished football team in the outer suburbs of south London.

31 *his Gold Medal* — the highest honour for amateur sportsmen or athletes, but Mick is unspecific about just how Sid acquired it.

31 *fiddle* — colloquial term for a violin.

31 *Your spitting image* — looking exactly like you.

31 *Married a Chinaman* — a legal impossibility.

31 *Choosy* — hard to please (colloquial).

32 *Shoreditch . . . Aldgate . . . Camden Town . . . Finsbury Park . . . Putney . . . Fulham . . . Caledonian Road . . . the Angel . . . Dalston Junction . . . Highbury Corner* — all these are districts in London, but quite distinct in location and social status.

32 *Nag's Head* — name of a public house (pub).

32 *a pitch* — a stall. The man was a street trader.

32 *dead spit of you* — exactly like you (see note for 'spitting image', p. 31).

32 *there was nothing in it* — the difference was unimportant.

33 *catch a draught* — Mick has combined two common ideas: to be in a draught and to catch a cold.

34 *up your arse* — up your bottom, backside (vulgar).

34 *a bloke I bumped into* — a man I met by chance.

34 *the Guildford by-pass* — a main road passing round Guildford, the chief town of Surrey, a county to the south of London.

34 *Fibber* — a liar. 'Fibber' is more usually applied to children, so is particularly belittling to Davies.

34 *I got the bullet* — (see note for P. 10).

34 *saved me from a punch up* — prevented me from getting into a fight.

35 *don't get perky* — don't be impudent, cheeky.

35 *Don't get out of your depth* — don't go too far, don't get involved in matters you don't understand.

35 *Keep your hands off my old mum . . . don't start taking liberties with my old mother* — keep off the subject of my mother . . . Treat her with respect.

35 *old rogue . . . old scoundrel* — rather old-fashioned terms for a dishonest man.

36 *you stink* — you smell offensive. (See p. 70 — Mick briefly withdraws that complaint, to humour Davies, but soon repeats it even more emphatically, p. 74.)

35 *You're an old skate* — (see note to p. 9).

35 *seven quid* — seven pounds (slang).

35 *Get a taker* — find someone to rent the room.

35 *in your range* — within your ability to pay.

35 *Rateable value ninety quid for the annum* — assessed for the purposes of local government taxation to be worth ninety pounds a year. Mick mixes together formal jargon ('rateable value' and 'annum') with very colloquial language ('quid').

35 *if you're all that keen* — if you are really determined and interested.

36 *trespassing, loitering with intent* — being on private property without the owner's permission, and standing about with the purpose of committing a crime when the occasion presents itself. These are the legal terms.

36 *daylight robbery* — flagrant and shameless exploitation of one person by another, immoral but not necessarily illegal. Mick has suddenly shifted from legalistic jargon, to a metaphor using the language of the law to mean something different. The effect is disturbing.

36 *filching* — petty stealing (slang).

36 *a number one decorator* — a first class house-painter.

36 *eight hundred odd* — a little more than eight hundred pounds.

36 *three thousand down* — three thousand pounds paid immediately in cash.

36 *no strings attached* — without demanding any special conditions.

36 *open and above board* — with complete honesty and straight-forwardness.

36 *family allowances* — a weekly payment made by the government to those parents with more than one child.

36 *remission of term for good behaviour* — a reduction of the prison sentence served by a convicted criminal which is earned by co-operative conduct towards the prison authorities.

36 *tea laid on* — cups of tea provided.

36 *comprehensive indemnity against Riot . . . Cattle* — a collection of the more dramatic events against which it is possible to buy insurance.

36 *to carry the can* — to bear the blame for a crime or mistake for which one is only partly responsible if at all.

36 *Who do you bank with* — with which bank do you have an account. An absurd question to ask Davies.

38 *Scrub it* — Stop it; forget it.

38 *Watch your step* — be careful about what you say and do.

38 *You're knocking at the door when no-one's at home* — you're wasting your time and energy.

38 *Don't overstep the mark, son* — don't go beyond the limits of courtesy and allowable behaviour. 'Son' merely emphasises Mick's sense of superiority.

39 *He's a bit of a joker, en'he?* — he enjoys playing practical jokes, doesn't he?

40 *knock up* — make something in a simple, rather slapdash way.

41 *I picked that bag up* — (see note to p. 16).

41 *they don't go far in the wintertime* — they don't last long; but also, they don't do much to keep you warm in winter.

41 *smoking-jacket* — a rather formal jacket, generally of velvet, at one time worn by wealthy or fashionable gentlemen in the evenings when they intended to smoke a pipe, cigars or cigarettes.

43 *someone after you?* — is there someone looking for you to hurt you?

43 *that Scotch git* — (see note to p. 9).

43 *any Harry* — a shortened form of the expression 'any Tom, Dick or Harry', meaning anyone at all, no matter how disreputable or unsuitable.

44 *I could be buggered* — I could be caught unawares, in trouble.

44 *they'd have me in* — they'd arrest me.

45 *the electrolux* — (see note to p. 6).

45 *spring cleaning* — an especially thorough cleaning, originally to celebrate the end of winter and the effective beginning of a new and brighter way of life.

45 *I gave it a good going over* — I cleaned every part of it carefully.

46 *gave you a start* — startled or alarmed you.

46 *to get up your nose* — as well as its literal meaning, appropriate enough here, the phrase can mean 'to annoy you'.

46 *a nominal sum* — a sum of money so small as to be hardly worth serious consideration.

46 *spiky* — awkward, unco-operative.

46 *I keep myself to myself* — I don't seek the company of others; I occupy myself with my own affairs.

46 *I been all over* — I've travelled widely, know what life is about.

46 *I can be pushed so far* — my patience should not be abused.

47 *You been playing me about* — you've been taking advantage of me, making a fool of me.

47 *got off on the wrong foot* — started off badly.

47 *Don't you pull anything* — don't try playing a mean trick on me.

48 *can't get the hang of him* — can't understand him.

48 *a man of the world* — a mature man with considerable experience of life.

49 *buckle down to* — apply himself seriously.

49 *he's a funny bloke* — he's a strange individual. 'Funny' can mean 'odd', 'unusual', 'not quite right', as well as 'amusing'. Mick chooses this moment to change his manner from friendliness to hostility, using the suggestion in Davies's remark that Aston is 'not quite right' (that is 'wrong in the head', mad) to justify his sudden aggressiveness.

50 *hypercritical* — unjustifiably critical.

50 *glib* — quick and insincere with words.

50 *keeping an eye on things* — making sure that nothing goes wrong.

50 *there's no getting away from that* — that's an undeniable fact.

50 *mess you about* — take advantage of you.

50 *in the services* — in one of the Armed Forces.

50 *serving . . . I was* — as well as the sense of 'serving' in the Armed Forces, there is the idea of 'serving' a prison sentence, which might be equally appropriate here.

50 *In the colonies* — this refers to the time when Britain was still an imperial power, governing territories in Africa and the East.

51 *deeds* — documents establishing ownership of property.

51 *references* — the names of reliable and responsible people who will be ready to vouch for the good character and suitability of a person applying for a job.

51 *like the back of my hand* — as if I saw it every day of my life; i.e. it is very familiar.

51 *I'm done* — I'm ruined.

51 *I'm waiting for the weather to break* — (see note to p. 16).

52 *that's shot it* — that's put an end to that possibility.

53 *Goldhawk Road* — in the Shepherd's Bush area of west London.

54 *the breaks* — the intervals allowed in the middle of the morning, at lunchtime and in the middle of the afternoon for workers to stop for refreshment.

55 *people started being funny* — people began to behave differently and strangely.

55 *I had something* — I had something wrong with me, a diagnosed illness.

55 *in your interests* — what is best for you.

55 *a minor* — not yet legally an adult.

56 *brought it up* — mentioned the subject.

56 *had a fit* — had a sudden attack of epilepsy, a seizure, a fit of hysterics.

56 *laid one of them out* — knocked one of the medical staff unconscious.

57 *laid everything out* — arranged everything in order. Traditionally, when someone in a family has died, the body is 'laid out' so that mourners may come to pay their last respects.

57 *steer clear of* — deliberately stay well away from.

Act III

59 *don't know where it's been* — this echoes the warning traditionally given by mothers to young children who are about to pick something up off the ground, perhaps to put in their mouths. It sounds comic coming from the tramp.

59 *it's not connected* — (see note to p. 26).

59 *them Blacks* — (see note to p. 13).

60 *can't get the hang of him* — (see note to p. 48).

60 *get this place going* — put it into working order.

60 *a penthouse* — a luxurious apartment at the top of a building, generally very expensive and sought after. Mick's whole speech is made up of phrases and images taken from the magazines and advertisements of the late fifties designed to appeal to the newly affluent, those people wanting to declare themselves as fashionable, well established and discriminating.

60 *teal-blue* — dark, greenish blue.

60 *offset* — have as a pleasing contrast to.

60 *afromosia teak veneer* — a thin layer of expensive-looking wood stuck over cheaper wood to create the appearance of affluence. The phrase itself has an exotic, lyrical quality that suits Mick's mood of rapturous daydreaming.

60 *a beech frame settee* — a sofa with the upholstery supported by a framework of beech wood.

60 *functional* — of starkly simple design, without additional decoration.

61 *Clobber* — useless objects which merely take up valuable space, most usually applied to old clothing and equipment.

61 *tuppence* — two pennies, in the old coinage; worth about one new penny. 'Wouldn't get tuppence for it' was a common way of indicating that something has no real value.

61 *You don't know where you are with him* — you can't be sure how to interpret his reactions; you don't know what he thinks of you.

62 *a bit of a lay down* — have a short rest. 'Lay' is substituted for 'lie' in a number of English dialects.

62 *haven't the foggiest idea* — have no idea at all.

62 *I've half a mind* — I'm almost ready to.

62 *give him a mouthful* — tell him forcefully what I think.

63 *I'm worn out* — exhausted.

63 *I got to move myself* — I must get myself organised, on my way.

63 *give you a hand* — help you.

63 *Everything laid on* — everything necessary for comfortable
-64 living provided.

65 *that puts the lid on it* — that finally ruins everything.

65 *The weather's dead against it* — weather conditions make it impossible (see pp. 16, 20, 51).

65 *getting on a while back* — some time ago now.

66 *off your nut* — out of your mind, crazy.

66 *mucking me about* — disturbing me and interfering with me.

66 *I've seen better days than you have* — I was once better off than you have ever been.

67 *one of them places* — a mental hospital.

67 *you keep your place* — don't try to appear better than you are, be more humble.

67 *a true pal* — an honest and reliable friend.

67 *Treating me like dirt* — (see note to p. 8).

67 *you got another think coming* — you're going to have to change your ideas.

67 *get the word* — be given the authorisation. Davies does not indicate who is likely to *give* the word, but the implication is that he believes Mick will.

67 *a creamer* — a lunatic (slang).

67 *you take my tip* — listen to me, pay attention.

67 *do your dirty work* — act as your servant.

67 *lousy, filthy hole* — disgusting, dirty, cramped room.

67 *up the creek* — out of your senses, mad, confused.

67 *You're half off!* — half crazy.

67 *Whoever saw you slip me a few bob* — (see note to p. 19).

67 *a nuthouse* — a mental hospital (slang).

68 *don't come nothing with me* — don't try getting violent with me.

68 *I don't think we're hitting it off* — I don't think we're getting on well together.

68 *a steady wage* — a reliable source of earned income, paid weekly.

68 *stinking shed* — worthless shed. Davies uses 'stinking' simply as a term of contempt, but Aston responds to its literal meaning, 'foul smelling', and throws that complaint back at Davies.

69 *I'LL STINK YOU* — the words themselves are nonsensical here, but they clearly convey the threat of violence, accompanied as they are by Davies's gesture with the knife.

70 *Tch, tch, tch* — sound indicating shocked disapproval.

70 *you ain't heard the last of this* — this isn't the end of the matter; I haven't given up.

70 *to sort him out* — to deal with him, make him co-operate.

70 *he's got a point, en he?* — he's right in one way.

71 *the sitting tenant* — he is paying rent and occupying the property, therefore has certain rights under the law. It is characteristic of Mick to use technical terminology whenever possible to impress and confuse Davies.

71 *it's a fine legal point* — it involves complicated and precise interpretations of the law.

71 *You get a bit out of your depth sometimes* — (see note to p. 35).

71 *as things stand* — considering the present state of affairs.

71 *having a go at doing up the place* — trying to redecorate the house.

71 *interior decorator* — a man who makes his living from painting and decorating the insides of houses.

72 *turn my hand to* — make an attempt at, try a new skill.

72 *to pick it up* — learn how to do it.

72 *you got the wrong man* — you've made a mistake, you're thinking of someone else.

72 *under a false impression* — deceived, mistaken.

73 *all this dirt* — all these lies.

73 *He's nutty* — he's mad (slang).

73 *half way gone* — more than half crazy.

74 *to put the old tin lid on it* — to make matters even worse.

74 *you stink from arse-hole to breakfast time* — you smell completely foul at all times (vulgar).

74 *pay you off* — give you a sum of money and dismiss you.

74 *half a dollar* — half a crown (slang). In old coinage this was worth two shillings and sixpence — equivalent to twelve and a half new pence.

74 *to chuck it in* — to give up my involvement in it.

75 *you been a mate to me* — you've been a good friend to me.

76 *yourn* — yours (dialect).

77 *Get it done in next to no time* — complete the task very quickly.

78 *they're working out all right* — they are proving quite adequate. Davies is finally reduced to a succession of hopeless, fragmented phrases of desperate appeal in the face of Aston's silence.